# Cambridge Elements ≡

Elements in the Economics of Emerging Markets
edited by
Bruno S. Sergi
*Harvard University*

# CROSS-BORDER INTERBANK CONTAGION RISK ANALYSIS

## Evidence from Selected Emerging and Less-Developed Economies in the Asia-Pacific Region

Roman Matousek
*Queen Mary University of London
and Universiti Utara Malaysia*

Ole Rummel
*The South East Asian Central Banks (SEACEN)
Research and Training Centre*

CAMBRIDGE
UNIVERSITY PRESS

# CAMBRIDGE
### UNIVERSITY PRESS

University Printing House, Cambridge CB2 8BS, United Kingdom

One Liberty Plaza, 20th Floor, New York, NY 10006, USA

477 Williamstown Road, Port Melbourne, VIC 3207, Australia

314–321, 3rd Floor, Plot 3, Splendor Forum, Jasola District Centre,
New Delhi – 110025, India

79 Anson Road, #06–04/06, Singapore 079906

Cambridge University Press is part of the University of Cambridge.

It furthers the University's mission by disseminating knowledge in the pursuit of
education, learning, and research at the highest international levels of excellence.

www.cambridge.org
Information on this title: www.cambridge.org/9781108794770
DOI: 10.1017/9781108882040

© Roman Matousek and Ole Rummel 2020

First published 2020

*A catalogue record for this publication is available from the British Library.*

ISBN 978-1-108-79477-0 Paperback
ISSN 2631-8598 (online)
ISSN 2631-858X (print)

# Cross-Border Interbank Contagion Risk Analysis

## Evidence from Selected Emerging and Less-Developed Economies in the Asia-Pacific Region

Elements in the Economics of Emerging Markets

DOI: 10.1017/9781108882040
First published online: July 2020

Roman Matousek
*Queen Mary University of London
and Universiti Utara Malaysia*

Ole Rummel
*The South East Asian Central Banks (SEACEN) Research and Training Centre*

**Author for correspondence:** Roman Matousek, r.matousek@qmul.ac.uk

**Abstract:** This Element provides a detailed overview of the structural changes in the Asia-Pacific region from the early 2000s onwards. It reviews the most relevant literature on this important topic. The following two research areas are explored: First, by deploying visual network analysis (VNA), we analyse cross-border interbank claims and liabilities of the individual countries located in the Asia-Pacific region. Such an analysis evaluates interbank exposures to systematically important banks within the specific market. The important advantage of VNA is that it allows us to examine the 'hierarchical' cross-country interbank contagion risk that seems to have been neglected in similar studies. Second, we evaluate the contagion risk for the individual countries spreading from the financial centres in Hong Kong, Singapore, Tokyo, New York and London. The analysis unveils links and statistical factors that could be used as a key tool for detecting the potential triggers of systemic risk.

**Keywords:** Asia-Pacific region, emerging economies, contagion risk

ISBNs: 9781108794770 (PB), 9781108882040 (OC)
ISSNs: 2631-8598 (online), ISSN 2631-858X (print)

# Contents

# 1 Introduction

A number of recent empirical studies by central banks and the academic literature have focused on the impact of the Great Financial Crisis (GFC) and the role of systematically important banks (SIBs) on the systemic stability of the financial system. These studies unambiguously show that cross-border interbank exposures affect the systemic stability of individual banking systems through the transmission of shocks – see, for example, Allen and Gale (2000), Haldane and May (2011), Yellen (2013) and Cerutti (2015), among others.

It is evident that contagion risk through cross-border interbank activities has not been easy to detect. The opaqueness of the linkages is even more pronounced when banks are linked through off-balance sheet financial activities. The complex financial cross-border interbank linkages conceal possible idiosyncratic shocks that may cause spillovers to other financial systems. Remolona and Shim (2015) showed the intensification of cross-border banking activity within the Asia-Pacific region after the GFC. Before the GFC, much of the cross-border activity in the region had been driven by US dollar credit intermediated largely by banks, which had origins in advanced economies. Banks within the Asia-Pacific region stepped in and dominated cross-border banking activity after the crisis. The rise in the intraregional trend was further boosted by the Association of Southeast Asian Nations (ASEAN) member governments that adopted a regional banking integration framework, with the aim of balancing the efficiency gains of regional integration against the risks of financial instability. The authors analysed the proliferation of regional bank branches and subsidiaries in the region, how these units funded themselves and what the implications were for their lending behaviour. They raised some specific issues relating to financial stability, vis-à-vis the potential for concentration of lending to a few creditors and systemic risks involving foreign branches, liquidity risks in foreign currency funding and the increasing share of short-term foreign currency loans in Asia-Pacific banks' intraregional lending.

The GFC shook the foundations of the international banking and financial system and put banks under immense stress. Cross-border bank lending proved to be one of the major financial channels through which stresses in the international financial system were transmitted to individual emerging markets and developing economies (Adekola and Sergi, 2016; Goyal et al., 2017; Takáts, 2018). During the GFC, cross-border lending by banks fell, affecting economies and banks that relied heavily on cross-border lending. The catch was that, although cross-border lending in US dollars declined, lending by international banks in local currencies increased in emerging markets and developing countries (Takáts, 2018). This indicated that foreign banks became major players in the domestic financial markets of most emerging markets and developing economies because they operated almost as local banks with foreign ownership and expanded their credits in local currencies. Other regions, like Central and Eastern Europe, continued to rely on cross-border lending that exposed their banking sector to risks such as currency mismatches (Takáts, 2018).

Since 2017, we have observed a faster growth in cross-border credit activities to non-bank financial borrowers in emerging and developing economies. The Asia-Pacific region exhibits substantial growth in financial flows since the GFC. These activities are positive elements for further sustainable growth in these regions. Nevertheless, this requires the implementation of macroprudential policy and liquidity management strategies by the financial regulators and central banks, in order to control systemic risk in financial markets.

As Genberg (2017) showed, cross-border financial integration in Asian emerging market economies (AEME) has become rather complex. Following a lengthy period of high economic growth, which has been primarily financed through bank lending, cross-border interbank linkages in the AEMA have a prominent global network component. On the one hand, this type of interconnectedness has a positive effect on the efficient allocation of funds in terms of innovation activities and competition. On the other hand, cross-border interconnectedness poses a higher contagion risk in terms of systemic instability within the banking system and financial institutions. Glasserman and Young (2015) further show that strongly interconnected financial systems report higher losses due to, and caused by, this contagion risk.

So far, empirical research on the systematic stability of the banking sector in AEME has been rather limited. It is imperative that financial regulators deploy models that allow them to monitor not only the soundness of SIBs but also the potential contagion risk caused by cross-country interbank linkages in AEME.

This Element provides a detailed overview of the structural changes in the Asia-Pacific region from the early 2000s onwards, and we also review the most relevant literature on this important topic. We shed light on the following two research objectives. First, we explore cross-border interbank claims and liabilities of the individual countries located in the Asia-Pacific region by deploying visual network analysis (VNA). Such an analysis evaluates interbank exposures to SIBs within the specific market. The important advantage of VNA is that it allows us to examine the 'hierarchical' cross-country interbank contagion risk that seems to have been neglected in similar studies. We evaluate the contagion risk to the individual countries spreading from the financial centres in Hong Kong, Singapore, Tokyo, New York and London. A number of studies have shown that network analysis is a suitable method for analysing the links between financial institutions (countries). It allows us to unveil links and statistical factors that could be used as a key tool for detecting the potential triggers of systemic risk and contagion effects. Overall, visual network analysis can capture the very extensive and complex interconnectedness of financial institutions (countries). The pros and cons of such a methodological approach have been extensively assessed in a number of studies published by academics and researchers from central banks, the International Monetary Fund (IMF) and the Bank for International Settlements (BIS) – for example, Allen and Gale (2000), Upper (2007), Chau-Lan et al. (2009), Espinosa-Vega and Sole (2010) and Changmo et al. (2014), among others.

Second, by creating a detailed mapping of cross-border interbank linkages in AEME, we may uncover possible weak links of an adverse credit event or liquidity contraction. Since we do not have data on SIBs through cross-border interbank linkages – as was applied, for example, by Upper (2007) – we will explore these links at the country level. The analysis should also provide some insights into potential idiosyncratic shocks, including the impact of 'home bias'. This type of analysis may identify whether the triggers of contagion risk are market shocks or country-specific shocks. We also address an important question regarding solvency and liquidity contagion risks. This is of crucial importance, and the findings may direct policymakers towards effective prudential management policies.

We use bilateral data on cross-border bank lending for twenty-eight countries. The sample includes nine global core countries (that is, the G7[1] plus Switzerland and Luxembourg), as well as six core economies in Southeast Asia and the Pacific region (namely, Australia, Hong Kong, Taiwan, South Korea, Macau and the Philippines). We further include thirteen periphery economies. The detailed discussion on data and methodology can be found in Section 4. The visual network analysis allows us to capture the dynamics and structural changes across these economies, including the Great Financial Crisis. Our analysis spans from 2000 Q4 to 2018 Q1.

We adopt the methodological framework proposed by Minoiu and Reyes (2013). The adoption of this methodological framework allows us to compare the findings for AEME with previous research and detect commonalities of the issues across economies. In addition, the execution of the model is relatively feasible, even for those who have little knowledge in the field of network simulations systems.

This Element contributes to current research in the following ways. To begin with, this is the first study that is exclusively focused on Asian-Pacific

---

[1] The Group of Seven (G7) countries include Canada, France, Germany, Italy, Japan, the United Kingdom and the United States.

economies, while taking into consideration the effect of the most developed countries and key financial centres. Second, the visual network analysis allows us to capture the flows of funds. This is a particularly important issue in the case of the liquidity constraint to which the financial institutions in the region were exposed during the financial crisis. A relatively long sample period of our analysis also helps us understand the significant structural changes that took place across the economies considered in our analysis. We further follow the weighted approach applied by Minoiu and Reyes (2013) to identify the potential intensity of capital flows across the selected economies.

Furthermore, our study provides both qualitive and quantitative analyses through VNA about cross-border contagion risk in seven selected Asian-Pacific economies. The key objective of such an analysis is to equip policy-makers with alternative scenarios of potential triggers of cross-border interbank contagion risk. An integral part of this analytical study is to provide recommendations on how to mitigate possible contagion risk within the specific economies and the Asia-Pacific region as a whole.

This comprehensive analytical overview allows the authors to identify some of the key problems that specific economies could face. In particular, they find that economies within the region surpassed the importance of many of the G7 countries (the United Kingdom and Japan, in particular). Since 2016, Hong Kong and China have dominated the regional financial system. This type of structural change will necessarily have implications for systemic stability not only in terms of regional stability but also on a global scale. The dominance of Hong Kong and its extensive links with China may be remarkable but perhaps not surprising. The authors argue that this extremely close link could have serious contagion effects if the Chinese economy were to face turbulence, mainly on account of the fact that international flows of money terminate in China and are not diversified further. This is very different from the 2000s, when Japan played the key role in the network. At that time, the flows of money from Japan were directed mainly towards Singapore, but Singapore in turn widely diversified the received financial resources. They conclude that there is a need to further explore economies' (banks') portfolio diversification in the region.

## 2 Systemic Changes in the Asia-Pacific Region: A Brief Overview

### 2.1 Systemic Changes in Asian Economies since 1997

Since the late 1990s, we have observed significant structural changes in terms of the systemic stability of financial markets. In particular, the activities of financial institutions have become more closely linked and interconnected. In 1997,

Asian countries experienced one of the most protracted crises in their recent history. The financial systems in many countries were nearly brought to a complete standstill. The crisis not only revealed significant structural problems in these countries' respective domestic economies but also showed the extensive interconnectedness of financial institutions in advanced economies and global financial centres. The lesson that financial markets learned during the Asian financial crisis was that domestic and/or external shocks can significantly undermine the systemic stability of the banking system if financial institutions are undercapitalized and face liquidity problems.

Nevertheless, there was a remarkable revitalization of the financial systems immediately after the crisis. That is in sharp contrast to what we saw during the GFC of 2007–8. One of the possible explanations why the GFC was much more severe and lasted for such a prolonged period was that since 1997, global financial markets have become even more 'integrated'. Emerging and less-developed economies have become extremely dependent not only on their own state of the economy but on the economic stability and the phase of the business cycles in advanced economies as well. This link could easily undermine their economic and financial stability and thus hinder their further development. The common lesson from the financial crises is that it is important to maintain sound macroeconomic fundamentals, along with financial stability underpinned by appropriate financial regulations. These are the basic measures that must be implemented by regulators and policymakers. Nevertheless, as we argue later, it is not sufficient that these measures focus only on the soundness of purely domestic markets. Bank or even systemic failures can be 'imported' through contagion effects from other countries. Anecdotal evidence further shows that these effects are not necessarily limited to geographically neighbouring countries but can be transmitted across continents.

The international bank lending market, which has substantially expanded in the last two decades, has become more vulnerable to external shocks. For example, in 2007, net cross-border bank lending stood at USD4.3 trillion. One year later, the same net cross-border lending was reduced to minus USD1 trillion. This was a consequence of financial market turbulence and uncertainty when the GFC fully unfolded. Such unprecedented volatility clearly indicates how financial liquidity can suddenly be reversed. Because of the complexity and extensive linkages across global financial markets, changes in one dominant financial market can have a significant knock-on effect on even relatively sound banking systems. This problem is more pronounced in emerging and less-developed economies that are more vulnerable to sudden inflows/outflows of short-term capital including speculative capital (Sergi, 2019). Furthermore, countries' extreme dependence on external finance, combined with an under-developed financial infrastructure and insufficient financial regulations, may lead to unfavourable conditions and an inability to withstand various forms of adverse effects. Such adverse effects can be further reinforced by the higher complexity of financial products. It has become more difficult to detect possible systemic risks within the financial system and/or across the financial systems. Ensuring the systemic stability of the banking system has thus become an imperative task for bank regulators.

## 2.2 The Asia-Pacific Region after the Great Financial Crisis

Emerging and less-developed economies in Southeast Asia have undergone significant structural changes in terms of their cross-border activities and financial exposures. Although they still rank rather low in terms of the volume of transferred funds, linkages with countries have changed. A general expansion of the volume of transactions is mostly due to the increased number of international banks that have established operations in these economies. Undoubtedly, these stylized facts can be regarded as an early benefit of the extensive linkages across banks in the Asia-Pacific region. These activities also reflect the banks' business strategy of diversifying their portfolio to limit potential risks. But increased cross-border financial linkages may have potential negative externalities in terms of systemic stability, including the case of sudden capital outflows that many countries have recently faced as a reaction to the phasing out of quantitative easing (QE) in the United States and Europe.

A number of studies have recently tried to identify the links between QE and capital flows to Asia (Onour and Sergi, 2010; Sergi et al., 2019). The outcomes are rather inconclusive. For example, Cho and Rhee (2013) argue that the first round of QE (QE1) substantially contributed to capital inflows to Southeast-Asian economies after the GFC. Their argument is based on the notion that QE1 lowered US yields, which 'helped' redirect capital flows to Asia. The authors do not share the view that QE2 and QE3 had similar effects as QE1. They also point to the housing market in some Asian economies and the fact that many residential house prices have risen sharply. It appears that housing prices went up in those economies where the domestic currency has not appreciated. These observations might also be ascribed to the prolonged QE policies and the resulting effects on global capital flows.

Overall, the turbulence in international financial markets during the GFC disrupted the flows of credit from advanced countries to emerging and less-developed economies in Asia and Latin America (Goyal and Sergi, 2015; Goyal et al., 2017). Based on the data from the BIS Banking Statistics, we observe a decline in cross-border claims, which undoubtedly had an adverse effect. This was mainly caused by a retrenchment by global and multinational financial institutions. The structural changes that financial institutions and financial markets have undergone in the last three decades or so caused financial markets at different stages of their development to react differently to external shocks.

## 3 Financial and Banking Systems in Selected Asia-Pacific Countries

### 3.1 Overview of the Philippine Banking System[2]

Since 1997, the Bangko Sentral ng Pilipinas (BSP) has implemented various regulatory reforms to enhance governance standards, expand risk-management systems, tighten disclosure and reporting requirements, increase minimum capitalization levels and improve compliance frameworks and systemic oversight. The BSP continues to promote mergers/consolidation through various mechanisms such as regulatory incentives and strengthening programmes, especially for the less-capitalized rural and cooperative banking sectors. The BSP has also demonstrated greater resolve in weeding out weak financial institutions by intensifying enforcement actions.

The BSP has worked for the adoption of international risk-based capital adequacy and disclosure standards (e.g., the Basel framework) since 2001. Commercial banks and their subsidiary banks and quasi-banks have been required to adopt enhanced standards ('Basel III') since 2014. Simpler standards ('Basel 1.5') apply to thrift, rural and cooperative banks that are not subsidiaries of commercial banks. The BSP has also adopted the international framework for dealing with domestic systemically important banks (basically banks considered too big to fail), requiring a staggered implementation of higher-capital buffers starting on 1 January 2017 towards full compliance by 1 January 2019.[3]

As Dizon et al. (2019) show, twelve new foreign banks have been approved to enter the Philippine market since the enactment of a July 2014 law liberalizing foreign participation in the banking sector; nine are operating and three are completing pre-operating requirements. Under the *ASEAN Economic Community (AEC) Blueprint*, the Philippines is working to help accomplish the goals of financial integration and work towards allowing the entry of qualified ASEAN banks (QABs) into the country. The BSP has concluded bilateral negotiations with the Central Bank of Malaysia on guidelines governing the entry of QABs into the two countries and has signed letters of intent with

---

[2] This section is based on Dizon et al. (2019), who provide a detailed survey of the current challenges.

[3] www.bsp.gov.ph/regulations/implementation.asp.

the central banks of Thailand and Indonesia to formalize discussions under the ASEAN Banking Integration Framework.

As of the end of February 2019, the banking sector comprised 46 universal and commercial banks, 54 thrift banks and 470 rural and cooperative banks, with combined assets of approximately USD319.7 billion (PHP16,682 billion). As Dizon et al. (2019) argue, commercial banks dominate the banking sector and account for around 91 per cent of the banking system's total resources. Twenty-one commercial banks (referred to as universal banks) have an expanded commercial banking license, which allows them to perform the functions of an investment house (such as securities underwriting) and invest in non-allied undertakings, in addition to regular commercial banking activities. A total of twenty-four banks (twenty commercial banks and four thrifts) are licensed to engage in additional derivatives activities. Of the twenty-six foreign banks in the Philippines, twenty-four are branches and two are majority foreign-controlled, domestically incorporated subsidiaries. Additionally, there are two offshore banking units (OBUs), as well as thirteen foreign bank representative offices, two of which are US banks as of April 2019.

More detailed regulations governing the operations of banks and other BSP-supervised financial institutions are available in various circulars, including the *Manual of Regulations for Banks*, *Manual of Regulations for Non-bank Financial Institutions* and *Manual of Regulations on Foreign Exchange Transactions*, compiled by the BSP.

The largest sectors comprising outstanding loans of the banking system as of the end of February 2019 were real estate activities (17.9 per cent), wholesale and retail trade (12.9 per cent), manufacturing (11.5 per cent) and households/consumers (11 per cent). Outstanding loans from banks' foreign currency deposit units stood at about USD16.6 billion at the close of 2018, mainly to resident borrowers such as merchandise exporters (17.7 per cent), public utilities (9.6 per cent) and producers/manufacturers (3.1 per cent).

The BSP is required by law to conduct regular examinations of its supervised financial institutions once every twelve months. Special examinations require the affirmative vote of at least five of the seven members of the BSP Monetary Board, the central bank's highest policy-making body. In addition, the BSP requires that bank financial statements are audited by BSP-accredited external auditors. External auditors are required to bring to the authorities' attention to any adverse audit findings and any material developments affecting the condition of its audited financial institutions. To promote independent and transparent auditing, the external auditor and/or auditing firms should be changed, or the lead and concurring partner should be rotated, at least every five years. A bank's senior management should also disclose to the BSP any significant risks or issues that may affect the bank, including changes in management.

Pending legislation in the Philippine Congress to amend the BSP's charter seeks to strengthen the BSP's supervisory and enforcement powers, provide legal protection for BSP officials and bank examiners in the performance of their official duties, enhance the BSP's ability to manage financial system liquidity (including authorization to issue its own securities) and allow for the resolution of troubled banks.

The deposit insurance scheme – administered by the Philippine Deposit Insurance Corporation (PDIC) – is patterned after the US Federal Deposit Insurance Corporation (FDIC). The PDIC has a permanent insurance fund (PIF) of about USD57 million (PHP3 billion), augmented by premiums paid by member banks (currently one-fifth of 1 per cent per annum of the deposit base). The PDIC's insurance coverage per depositor is approximately USD9,600 (PHP500,000).

Revisions to the PDIC charter in 2004, 2009 and 2016 enhanced the PDIC's receivership, liquidation and resolution powers. Among others, the most recent amendments allow early intervention in problem banks before closure, simplify the payout of insurance coverage to affected depositors and provide a more seamless transition from closure to liquidation.

The Philippine banking system (PBS), which represents the core of the financial system in the Philippines, is classified into the following categories: universal and commercial banks (U/KBs), thrift banks (TBs) and rural and cooperative banks (RCBs).[4] U/KBs represent the largest group of financial institutions in the PBS, which also offer the widest variety of banking services. TBs are composed of savings and mortgage banks, private development banks, stock savings and loan associations and microfinance thrift banks. The number of U/KBs and their TBs subsidiaries comprise 9.2 per cent of the 585 total number of operating banks' head offices. As of the end of March 2018, U/KBs still dominated the Philippine banking sector, holding PHP15,333 billion in total assets, or 90.8 per cent of the banking system's total assets. Likewise, the loan portfolio of U/KBs took up 88.9 per cent of the total banking system's portfolio and represented 49.5 per cent of nominal gross domestic product (GDP).

---

[4] Rural banks and cooperative banks are differentiated from each other by ownership. Rural banks are privately owned and managed, while cooperative banks are organized/owned by cooperatives or federations of cooperatives.

For the purposes of having a broader view of the PBS, universal banks are classified further into three types: (1) private domestic banks (PDBs), (2) government banks and (3) foreign bank branches (FBBs). Likewise, commercial banks are classified further into three types: (1) PDBs, (2) foreign bank subsidiaries (FBS) and (3) FBBs. Most of the FBBs and subsidiaries, which can be both universal and commercial, originate from the Asia-Pacific region. In particular, some 57.9 per cent of FBBs and subsidiaries originate in countries within the Asia-Pacific region.

Meanwhile, the Basel Committee on Banking Supervision (BCBS) has developed a methodology for assessing the systemic importance of banks using an indicator-based approach with different categories. According to the BCBS, a bank's size is a key measure of its systemic importance (BIS, 2011). Aside from bank size, other indicators include interconnectedness, substitutability and complexity. However, countries may adopt new methodologies, introduce new indicators and/or vary the weights of factors in identifying the domestic SIBs (D-SIBs) based on the BCBS's assessment.

Dizon et al. (2019) illustrate the use of the BCBS's indicator for interconnectedness with other financial institutions. Individual indicators of interconnectedness, by BCBS' definition, are composed of intra-financial system assets (IFS assets), intra-financial system liabilities (IFS liabilities) and the wholesale funding ratio. IFS assets of U/KBs, such as debt securities issued by financial institutions (held by the bank) and loans (from the bank) to financial institutions, are largely attributed to universal PDBs, which have an 81.8 per cent share in the total for U/KBs.

The significant share of domestic banks at 90 per cent (PDBs of U/KBs, as well as government banks) in terms of size suggests that domestic banks could channel contagion to other resident banks through their investment in debt securities, the extension of loans and the acceptance of deposits. Negative externalities in the financial system may trigger a spillover effect in the domestic banking system once these risks materialize. Moreover, assessing the interbank linkages through the assets and liabilities side of a bank's balance sheet could be indicative of the degree of susceptibility to a contagion effect, as negative shocks can be transmitted from countries or regions to the domestic market.

The aforementioned indicators provide an overview of the U/KBs' systemic importance in the financial system. However, in order to further assess the contagion and effects of possible spillovers following a failure of a group of banks' counterparties, a more detailed study on the cross-border exposures of these banks is necessary. These are discussed in the sections that follow.

## 3.2 The Banking Sector in South Korea[5]

In South Korea, there are 148 licensed banks, consisting of 52 commercial banks, five specialized banks and 91 mutual savings banks. Banks in South Korea are regulated by the Financial Supervisory Service (FSS), which is responsible for examining and supervising financial institutions under the broad oversight of the Financial Services Commission (FSC). Five commercial banks play key roles: Shinan, Nonghyup, KB, Hana and Woori.

Shinhan Financial Group was the first bank in South Korea, founded under the name Hanseong Bank in 1897. The bank operates through its retail banking, corporate banking, international banking and other banking segments. Headquartered in Seoul, it manages 871 branches and 27 private wealth management service centres in South Korea, as well as 14 branches in other countries. The bank employs around 13,400 staff, and total assets of the bank are around USD340 billion.

NongHyup Financial Group, created from the merger of Agricultural Bank and Agricultural Federation, was founded in 1961. The group provides financing, mortgages, personal lines of credit, corporate finance, real estate finance and new technology finance services. It also offers life, property and casualty insurance products. Headquartered in Seoul, the bank employs around 13,000 staff, and the bank's total assets amount to USD315 billion.

KB Financial Group, also headquartered in Seoul, is a financial holding company that offers financial services through its subsidiaries. The group operates through various business segments: retail banking, corporate banking, other banking, credit cards, investment and securities; and life insurance operations. While the corporate banking operations consist of corporate banking services, the group's other banking operations include treasury activities and back-office administrative operations. The investment and securities operations include securities brokerage, investment banking, securities investment and trading, and other capital market services. The life insurance segment comprises life insurance and wealth management services. The bank has reported total assets of USD275 billion.

Hana Financial Group was created in 1971 and is headquartered in Seoul. The bank offers mergers and acquisitions, corporate finance, fundraising, risk management advisory and securities trading and underwriting services. Total assets of the bank were USD308 billion.

Finally, Woori Financial Group provides commercial banking products and services to individual customers, small- and medium-sized enterprises and major corporations in South Korea. It provides consumer banking, corporate banking,

---

[5] Lee (2019) provides a more thorough analysis of the current issues and challenges in the South Korean banking sector.

capital markets and investment banking among other activities. Woori Bank is a part of Woori Financial Group and has 894 branches in South Korea and 22 branches internationally. The bank's total assets amount to USD296 billion.

As Lee (2019) shows, banks in South Korea can be classified into two categories: commercial banks and specialized banks. Commercial banks consist of nationwide and local banks and branches of foreign banks. As for special banks, these are defined as banks that were established under special act rather than the universal Banking Act and include the Korea Development Bank, Industrial Bank of Korea, Korea Eximbank and Suhyup Bank. Their main business models can differ from those of commercial banks because they were founded to finance and manage special projects of sectors that could suffer from insufficient access to funding by commercial banks only. The four largest-ranked financial institutions in terms of bilateral transaction volumes are domestic banks, securities companies, investment funds and trusts. While branches of foreign banks have connections with other sectors, domestic banks play an important role within the Korean financial sectors. Figure 6 shows the interconnectedness of the banking sector based on mutual transactions among domestic banks. It includes nineteen domestic banks, comprising nationwide and local commercial banks and special banks, and identifies six D-SIBs. By contrast, the D-SIBs identified by the Financial Services Commission in 2019 included four bank holding companies (Shinhan Financial Group, Hana Financial Group, KB Financial Group and NH Financial Group) and one bank (Woori Bank). It is important to note that the Korean banking sector receives overseas funding conditions with relatively low levels of credit-default swaps (CDS).[6]

Lee (2019) argues that the banking sector has remained stable with enough capacity for withstanding domestic and external shocks. However, there were considerable uncertainties that can put pressure on the Korean economy and financial sector. In particular, the monetary policy normalization of central banks in the major countries and protectionism can be detrimental factors heightening uncertainties. Therefore, it is necessary to focus on the potential external risks that may threaten financial stability and how the cross-border financial network affects the transmission of such risks to the domestic banking system.

### 3.3 The Banking System in Indonesia[7]

The financial system in Indonesia is mostly dominated by banks, compared to other financial institutions. Banks control around 90 per cent of the national loan

---

[6]  A credit default swap is a financial swap agreement that the seller of the CDS will compensate the buyer in the event of a debt default or other credit event.

[7]  An extensive discussion about current issues in the Indonesian banking system can be found in Muhajir et al. (2019).

market share. In 2018, the Indonesian banking system had 115 commercial banks that included state-owned banks, private banks, development banks and foreign branch banks. Besides these, there were also 1,607 rural banks, which function as economic drivers for the small- and medium-sized enterprise (SME) segment.

Despite the large numbers of banks, the banking market in Indonesia is dominated by some of the large banks, a fact that is becoming an issue for institutions that are 'too big to fail' (TBTF). Taking this into account and as one of the G20 member countries, the financial regulator in Indonesia has conducted financial reforms by addressing the TBTF issue and strengthening the resilience of financial institutions. One of them is by adopting the global systemically important bank (G-SIB) methodology assessment recommended by BCBS (2011) and applying it to the domestic level by identifying domestic systemically important banks (DSIB).

The stipulations concerning systemic banks are stated in Article 1 of the *Financial System Prevention and Crisis Management Act*. Systemic banks are banks that, due to the size of their assets, capital and liabilities, the broad network or transaction complexity of banking services and any linkages with other financial sectors or some other banks or financial services sectors, would have a significant operational or financial impact if the banks were impaired or even fail. Under these rules, especially regarding interconnectedness, calculations for cross-border activity are not included. Interconnection is calculated only for the level of the domestic banking system.

Muhajir et al. (2019) argue that the Indonesian banking industry experienced a challenging period in 2015 and 2016. This was primarily because of a downturn in macroeconomic conditions that included lower commodity and oil and gas prices. These factors resulted in an overall increase in non-performing loan rates and restructured loans across multiple sectors in banks' portfolios. Despite these challenges, the banking sector showed signs of growth, although Indonesian banks have been more cautious in disbursing new loans; therefore, overall loan growth in 2016 slowed down in comparison with previous years.

As Muhajir et al. (2019) show, the Jokowi Administration initiated thirteen new stimulus packages between 2015 and March 2017 to promote economic growth and stabilize the banking sector. In addition to these stimuli, a tax amnesty program was also initiated. The key objectives of the tax amnesty program are to increase tax income, improve taxpayers' compliance rates and pull more offshore assets back into Indonesia. There are three phases in the program, and the tax authorities managed to collect IDR107 trillion in penalty payments by the end of the second phase.

Bank Indonesia (BI) has played an important role in supporting economic growth by reducing its policy rate gradually from 7.5 to 6.5 per cent in June 2016. BI has also changed its benchmark rate to the BI seven-day repo rate to reduce the disparity between the BI rate and the interbank rate. Loan and deposit rates have decreased since then; however, the overall net interest margin of commercial banks has remained stable.

BUKU 3- and BUKU 4-category banks (i.e., those banks with capital of more than USD385 million) have benefited from the decrease in the BI rate, as they have been able to gain more loan and third-party deposit market share, whereas the decreasing market share of BUKU 1- and BUKU 2-category banks has created a need for consolidation. A number of merger and acquisition transactions were closed as the challenging environment led to lower business valuations that brought more opportunities to investors. The acquisition of Bank Windu Kentjana International by China Construction Bank Corporation, as well as the merger of Bank Metro Express and Centratama National Bank to become Shinhan Bank Indonesia, were two of the transactions that were closed in the last two years. In addition to these deals, Cathay Financial Holding acquired a 15 per cent stake in Mayapada Bank, with a total value of IDR1.7 trillion.

As reported in Muhajir et al. (2019), the interbank money market between cross-border banks in Indonesia faced a significant decline after the GFC. The magnitude of net cross-border interbank transactions reached its lowest level of USD21.23 million in 2008, compared to the previous year which saw USD23.78 million. Anecdotal evidence suggests that constricting cross-border activity at that time was very much felt in the Asian region.

The GFC has shown that especially for emerging countries like Indonesia, the transmission of external factors such as spillover risk from other countries can happen due to the linkages of cross-border financial institutions. As such, international banks constitute a contagion risk to the Indonesian banking system which should be anticipated early on.

The growth of the cross-border interbank money market began to revive and the amount of transactions in the interbank money market in 2017 was the highest for the last ten years. This fact is motivated by increasing liquidity flows from emerging countries to advanced countries as a result of growing export-import trading activity in recent years.

For the cross-border interbank money market, the interconnection of banks in Indonesia and other banking systems occurs mostly with countries regarded as financial hubs in the region. Singapore dominates the proportion of the interbank money market as the country that has the most transactions with banks from Indonesia. Furthermore, Hong Kong and UK banks constitute the second- and third-largest connections respectively. Nonetheless, these data do not yet differentiate between the origin of the bank or the home country; for instance, the Singapore branch of Sumitomo is assumed to represent Sumitomo Bank Japan, or Deutsche Bank Singapore Branch is assumed to represent Deutsche Bank Germany and so on.

## 3.4 Financial Sector Development in Papua New Guinea[8]

The financial sector in Papua New Guinea (PNG) is rather small in terms of the number of financial institutions. The system is dominated by four key commercial banks that account for 94 per cent of total financial sector assets. As for their ownership, two banks are domestic (Bank South Pacific (BSP) and Kina Bank), and two banks are foreign institutions from Australia (Australia and New Zealand Bank (ANZ) and Westpac). In addition, there are twelve licensed financial institutions in PNG that include microfinance institutions and small firms that provide personal loans. The financial system also includes twenty-two savings and loans societies. That said, concentration is a reality. The dominant position is held by BSP, which has 55.4 per cent of total loans outstanding in the market, against ANZ's 26.6 per cent, Westpac's 14.3 per cent and Kina Bank's 3.7 per cent. In terms of branches in PNG, BSP has 44 branches, as well as 45 sub-branches, 307 ATMs and 178 agents. That compares with Westpac's 16 branches, ANZ's 16 and Kina Bank's 4. Finally, Nationwide Microbank (MiBank) has 12 branches.

The financial system includes banks, savings and loans societies, superannuation funds, finance companies, micro-banks and life insurance companies. The overarching goal of a supervisory and regulatory function is to maintain a sound market-based financial system and risk-based supervision to achieve the stability objectives of the Bank of PNG. As part of its regulatory and supervisory roles, the Bank of PNG issues licenses to the banks and other financial institutions to conduct banking and other financial services in PNG.

The Bank of PNG is fully in charge of licensing banks and the minimum regulatory requirements for obtaining a bank license are explicitly listed. These requirements include a minimum capital requirement; banks pay around USD4.6 million, while for a financial company, it takes USD0.46 million to obtain a license to operate. Further supplementary regulatory requirements are that the banks' executive managers have to meet the 'fit and proper' requirement.

Aba (2019) stresses that the key and fundamental objective of the Bank of PNG, as the regulator, is to maintain the stability of the financial system in PNG. The PNG financial system is a key economic agent in PNG by being worth over

---

[8] Aba (2019) provides a detailed overview of the financial markets in Papua New Guinea.

50 per cent of PNG's GDP. This large share requires that stability is maintained to secure its integrity and the health of the PNG economy. The Bank of PNG has full responsibility for off- and on-site regulatory activities. The organizational structure of banking supervision and regulation under the Bank of PNG is such that it promotes systemic stability. It should allow the implementation of such policies that can detect systemic problems within the banking system in the early stages and prevent them from propagating to become possible triggers of a financial crisis. The Bank of PNG also ensures that the financial and operational soundness of banks and financial companies is maintained; that the interest of depositors, superannuation contributors and holders of life insurance policies are protected; and that the general stability of the whole financial system is maintained to generate confidence about the financial system and the economy.

As noted previously, the banking system is concentrated into four commercial banks and a number of micro-banks. BSP, a locally owned bank, is the largest, with branches and agents right across the country and the Pacific region in Fiji, Samoa, Tonga, Solomon Islands, Cook Islands, Vanuatu and a subsidiary in Cambodia. ANZ and Westpac are subsidiaries of Australian-based banks, while Kina Bank is a new foreign bank, which bought out Maybank in 2015. The micro-banks are very small players in the financial market.

As argued by Aba (2019), the main challenges that the banking sector currently face are the lack of foreign currency and trading in the interbank foreign exchange market. This is caused by the growing demand for foreign currency as a reaction to increased import activities that is further strengthened by lower prices of export commodities and the lower volume of foreign direct investment (FDI). At the same time, banks show excess liquidity in local currency in the domestic banking system, which is explained by the limited number of business opportunities. Since banks have reached their exposure limits on lending to certain sectors of the economy, this excess liquidity is distributed unevenly across the banks.

Despite these challenges, banks have been performing strongly with very large profits (Aba, 2019). Arguably, the profits from their operations in PNG subsidize the costs of other branches in the Pacific. Their balance sheets are healthy, with positive net assets. Adequate capital is maintained, and credit is also growing and is extended to all sectors of the economy. While lending to some sectors like real estate dropped, home and personal loans increased, offsetting the fall in real estate and commercial lending. However, credit as a fraction of GDP has fallen since April 2013. Declines in bank credit, GDP growth, commodity prices and interest and exchange rates are seen as shocks to domestic banks' activities and can escalate to contagion in the banking network. For example, a liquidity shortage faced by a SIB both in the foreign exchange and domestic markets can lead to shortages in other banks that can spread and infect other healthy banks.

## 3.5 The Malaysian Banking System[9]

The Malaysian financial system has started consolidation and restructuring to reduce its fragmentation. These structural changes were the reflection of the financial crisis in Southeast Asia in 1997. Bank Negara Malaysia (BNM) proposed the consolidation through the merger and acquisition of Malaysia's local banking institutions into ten key banks. The consolidation and restructuring were successfully achieved in 2002. The objective was to enhance the ability of the banking sector to withstand the competitive pressures from international banks. BNM is in charge of licensing and regulating commercial banks, investment banks, Islamic banks and money brokers.

Sababathy and Ling (2019) show that as a result of the early restructuring, the Malaysian banking sector is well-developed and diversified, with a wide range of domestic and foreign financial institutions. The banking system comprises twenty-seven commercial banks (eight domestic and nineteen foreign), sixteen Islamic banks (ten domestic and six foreign) and eleven investment banks. Commercial banks are the largest provider of funds, performing retail banking services, including acceptance of deposits, supplying loans and providing payment and remittance services. Islamic banks conduct a similar range of banking activities based on Shariah principles. Meanwhile, investment banks are responsible as financial intermediaries for capital market activities such as dealing in securities, raising capital and security underwriting, besides providing corporate advisory services. In terms of financing, the banking system has about MYR1.6 trillion in outstanding loans, equivalent to more than 117 per cent of GDP at the end of 2017.

Considerable efforts have been undertaken to strengthen the resilience of the banking system over the last decade, particularly in the aftermath of the Asian Financial Crisis. Realizing the need for stronger and larger domestic financial institutions, an industry-wide restructuring and consolidation programme was introduced by BNM in 1999. This has successfully reduced fragmentation and transformed the banking industry to better equip it with enhanced capacity to serve the domestic economy. The seventy-seven domestic banking institutions that existed in the 1980s have merged to form eight main domestic banking groups under the consolidation programme. As highlighted previously, the five largest domestic commercial banks in Malaysia now account for 70 per cent of

---

[9] This Section is based on Sababathy and Ling (2019).

total banking system assets. Five out of the eight domestic banking groups have also expanded regionally and emerged as key players within the ASEAN region.

Although banks in advanced economies faltered during the GFC – with some ending in bankruptcy – the Malaysian banking system remained resilient, with sound profitability levels and ample capital buffers to absorb shocks in the event of future stressed events. At the end of 2017, the capital ratios of all banks were well above the regulatory minima. More than 75 per cent of capital was in the form of the highest-quality loss-absorbing instruments, which included equity, retained earnings and reserves, allowing banks to withstand macroeconomic and financial shocks without adversely affecting financial intermediation. A series of macroprudential measures implemented since 2010 strengthened the risk management practices of banks and also further mitigated potential risks by reducing banks' exposures to over-leveraged households (BNM, 2017), thus improving the asset quality of banks to a low of 1.1 per cent liquidity coverage ratio (LCR). In addition, requirements for the banking institutions as part of the Basel III reform package have been phased in since June 2015, which required all banks to maintain sufficient high-quality liquid assets at a minimum of 100 per cent[10] of total projected net cash outflows for the next thirty days. Banks have all transitioned smoothly to this requirement.

Sababathy and Ling (2019) argue that the nature and extent of financial linkages of the Malaysian banking system have evolved and increased steadily since the GFC. The external exposures of Malaysian banks are relatively low and account for only 10 per cent of total assets in 2017. Banks' claims on, and liability obligations to, non-resident counterparties grew at a compounded annual growth rate of 11.9 and 12.2 per cent, respectively, since 2008. The rapid expansion of Malaysian banks' external exposures is affected by two factors. The first is the sizeable presence of foreign banks in Malaysia, including operations in the Labuan International Banking and Financial Centre (LIBFC). LIBFC, established in 1990, is an offshore financial centre that offers tax incentives for financial and capital market activities. In lieu of this, LIBFC banks' role as a booking centre is prominent, as onshore banks, primarily domestic banking groups, conduct their foreign-currency intermediation activities via their Labuan offices. The second factor is the regionalization of domestic banks, particularly in the ASEAN region. The external exposures are in the form of (i) intra-group transactions between banks and related offices abroad in the form of interbank placements and borrowings and capital funds,

---

[10] The LCR requirement was phased-in from June 2015, with an initial transitional requirement of 60 per cent. Full compliance of the 100 per cent requirement is in effect starting 1 January 2019.

(ii) deposits accepted from non-residents, and (iii) loans extended to non-resident counterparties.

The low risk profile of banks' external exposures is discussed in BNM's *Financial Stability Review 2018*. Malaysian banks are more exposed to adverse market and geopolitical developments across different economies, particularly within Asia. This is a consequence of the rapid growth and profile of banks' cross-border exposures. Moderate spillover effects were felt in the domestic market during periods of tightened US dollar conditions in 2008, which is reflected in the increased spreads of onshore USD/MYR cross-currency swap rates and the widening of short-term US dollar liquidity mismatch positions of banks in Malaysia (BNM, 2013). As a result of the increasing participation of foreign investors, domestic financial markets have become increasingly susceptible to volatile two-way portfolio flows induced by such regional and global developments. This has added to further concerns about banks' external debts, which are predominantly in the form of short-term instruments such as deposits and interbank transactions and have evoked concerns of banks also being susceptible to sudden withdrawal shocks.

Sababathy and Ling (2019) summarise that in terms of the Islamic banking activities, Malaysia launched Islamic banking in August 2006. This was done under the umbrella of the newly established Malaysian International Islamic Financial Centre (MIFC) that has the objective to be a leading Islamic banking institution. In the early stages of development, the government set up incentives to engage banks to operate in the Islamic finance market. Currently, there are eighteen Islamic Malaysian and foreign banks that conduct Islamic banking activities in Malaysia. Islamic banking is fully compatible with Sharia law.

## 3.6 The Indian Banking System[11]

The banking system in India has undergone complex transformation over the last five decades. In 1991, the first so-called Narasinham Committee on Financial Sector Reforms launched the programme of necessary reforms. The changes focused on the deregulation of the banking sector – particularly credit control allocations, along with interest rate controls on deposit and loans. The banking sector was also gradually opened to new entrants – private and foreign banks. An integral part of this reform was an extensive recapitalization of state-owned banks. Herd et al. (2010) noted that INR204 billion was spent overall on banking consolidation during the 1990s, which corresponds to 1.5 per cent of GDP in 2009.

---

[11] This Section is based on Sharma (2019), who provides a detailed overview of the Indian banking system.

As Sharma (2019) shows, the second stage of reforms reflected the recommendations of the second Narasinham Committee on Financial Sector Reforms in 1998. These changes aimed to restore the stability of the banking system through improved banking regulation (imposing minimum standards on capital adequacy) and increase competitiveness and efficiency. As a consequence of these measures, there has been a wave of mergers and acquisitions among banks. Some of these were conducted on market principles, but in many cases, the government 'assisted' in this consolidation process.

Herd et al. (2011) argued that the government would have to continue the recapitalization of the banking sector, and about eighteen to twenty public sector banks (PSBs) would require further financial assistance. As for the privately owned banks, it was also expected that additional capital was needed in order to stabilize particularly small-sized private banks. Herd et al. (2011) showed that the government prepared the provision of INR165 billion for the recapitalization of PSBs in the 2010–2011 budget. These were additional resources to the already used INR31 billion in the period from 2008 to 2009.

Sharma (2019) argues that the cost of the restructuring programme that involved bank recapitalizations, debt recovery and gradual privatization reached 2 per cent of GDP over the period from 1993 to 1999. The bulk of poor-quality assets on the balance sheet had been written off. However, new non-performing loans (NPLs) – close to 2.5 per cent of GDP – have been accumulated in 2010. This problem is reinforced by the fact that the provisions against NPLs were only 46 per cent in 2010. The regulator responded to the low level of provisions by increasing provisioning requirements to 70 per cent by the end of 2010. The current level of NPLs could eventually cause a systemic risk in the sector, unless the government steps in. It is evident that the balance sheets of PSBs have again gradually deteriorated particularly in terms of outstanding loans.

The administrative regulation of Indian banks substantially reduced competitiveness pressures. In terms of total assets, the market share of state-owned banks was more than 90 per cent. Such a deformed market structure marginalized activities of private and foreign commercial banks. The lack of market pressures and competition led to an inefficient credit allocation by state-owned commercial banks. This was later reflected in the deterioration of bank balance sheets. In particular, there has been an increase in the volume of NPLs; bank profitability dropped and, consequently, banks became undercapitalized. At the end of the 1980s and the beginning of the 1990s, it became evident that major qualitative reforms of the banking sector were necessary in order to avoid the collapse of the sector.

The Indian banks were, until very recently, universal in their activities. However, the sector has now been opened to differentiated banks that serve niche clients/segments. The first step in this direction was made by issuing licenses to small-finance and payment banks, which commenced their operations during the last two years. The idea of setting up wholesale and long-term finance banks is being mooted as well, which will be entrusted with the task of meeting the credit needs of the infrastructure sector and small, medium and corporate businesses. It is envisaged that differentiated banks will contribute to the economic development by furthering the cause of financial inclusion and catering to varied credit needs in the country.

Sharma (2019) further illustrates that, more recently, the banking sector in India is facing challenges of asset quality concerns and weak balance sheets. The ratio of gross non-performing assets (NPAs) as a percentage of gross advances has increased in recent years, with the ratio of gross NPAs being much higher in PSBs as compared to private-sector banks (PvSBs). Further, the concentration of NPAs remains proportionally higher in the industrial sector vis-à-vis the agriculture and service sectors The current NPA issue has been variously attributed to excessive credit growth in the preceding period, long-term infrastructure financing by banks leading to asset-liabilities mismatches, unfavourable economic conditions and structural issues negatively impacting the funded projects (Samantaraya, 2016; Sengupta and Vardhan, 2017). The capital-to-risk-weighted assets ratio for PSBs was 11.7 per cent, whereas for PvSBs, it was equal to 16.4 per cent as of March 2018 (Reserve Bank of India, 2018b). The Insolvency and Bankruptcy Code, as discussed later, is one of the most important steps taken by policymakers to not only tackle the present episode but also ensure that the resolution process becomes efficient so as to minimize the risk of such incidences occurring in future.

The problem of worsening asset quality in India was compounded by the multiplicity of legal acts and processes, their complexity, as well as their improper utilization by the banks, which made the recovery and resolution process difficult in case of bad loans (Reserve Bank of India, 2017b). A landmark development was the introduction of the Insolvency and Bankruptcy Code in 2016, which has now become a single law for insolvency and bankruptcy in a time-bound manner and envisages the speedy resolution of bad assets, bringing much-needed efficiency to the process.

The recapitalization of PSBs in view of their weak balance sheets and the impact on fresh credit creation is one of the important steps in solving the ongoing problem of asset quality. The majority ownership of the government in these banks, however, continues to limit their access to market resources for raising capital (Sengupta and Vardhan, 2017). At the same time, recapitalization by the government imposes huge costs on the public exchequer. Keeping these trade-offs in mind, the Indian government recently introduced a recapitalization package named the *Indradhanush* programme.

The consolidation of public sector banks in the banking sector has long been an issue in the policy discourse, with the various committees formed by the policymakers arguing for the same (Narasimham Committee Report, 1991 and 1998). The government of India has since embarked on the route of consolidation of public sector banks. The first step was the merger of the State Bank of India (the largest bank in India) with its associate banks, which went into effect in 2017. There is a proposal to merge three more PSBs together to form the second-largest bank in the near future.

Indian banks, serving an emerging nation, are entrusted with a multitude of developmental activities as well. Financial inclusion is one such goal, which has been pursued continuously over the years to bring the hitherto unbanked part of the population under the ambit of the formal banking sector. As Sharma (2019) shows, the ever-changing and evolving banking landscape in India continues to give impetus to India's growth story.

### 3.7 The Structure of the Banking System in Vietnam[12]

In the transition economy of Vietnam, the financial market is dominated by the banking sector; therefore the government and the State Bank of Vietnam (SBV) have undertaken a decade-long reform effort and strict efficiency measures to better direct the banking system towards more sustainable development. Nguyễn et al. (2019) argue that the sector experienced significant structural and operational changes since the 'Doi Moi' economic reforms initiated in 1986. According to the World Bank, the Vietnamese banking sector has significantly contributed to the country's successful economy as a rising tiger in Southeast Asia. Despite fundamental reforms and a dramatic expansion in banking, the system has still suffered structural fragility, especially during and after the GFC. More specifically, several problems have emerged (e.g., a proliferation of bad debts, weak balance sheets and under capitalization, interrelated ownership and lending, and a deterioration in competitiveness). In 2012, SBV introduced a comprehensive restructuring scheme to improve banking performance and sustainability towards the financial integration associated with the pillars set by the AEC and the Trans-Pacific Partnership. In this context, Vietnamese banking efficiency has attracted great attention not only from

---

[12]  Nguyễn et al. (2019) provide an overview of the most recent changes in the Vietnamese financial system.

academics but also from policymakers as they look to boost competitive power and bring the banking system up to par with other countries in the region.

Nguyễn et al. (2019) argue that the system has undergone significant and prolonged reforms over the past three decades, moving towards the banking modus operandi that closely resembles those of other emerging markets and newly industrialized economies. After the 'Doi Moi' economic reforms in 1986, the banking industry changed from a mono into a two-tier system, in which each tier specializes in different roles and responsibilities. The first tier is the SBV, managing monetary policy, stabilizing the value of the currency and governing the healthy operation of commercial banks. The central bank has achieved a certain degree of independence as defined by Sergi (2000). The second tier includes commercial banks and non-bank financial institutions, providing a variety of banking and financial services. The commercial banking sector comprises a diverse mix of players, ranging from relatively large state-owned commercial banks (SOCBs) down to tiny privately-held banks. However, the system is dominated by the four large SOCBs, accounting for about 50 per cent of total assets in the system. Their branch network covers nearly all provinces and big cities in Vietnam. Except for Vietnamese banks for social policies and branches of foreign banks, the sector is classified into four groups: SOCBs, joint-stock commercial banks (JSCBs), wholly foreign-owned banks (FOBs) and joint-venture banks (JVBs).

As Nguyễn et al. (2019) discuss, the period before the GFC from 2000 to 2007 witnessed a remarkable expansion in the Vietnamese banking sector, not only in terms of the burgeoning number of banks but also the remarkable expansion in total assets and capital. This period was associated with the deregulation and financial liberalization marked by a more relaxed regulatory regime that included the removal of interest rate controls. Next came the opening of the local market to foreign entrants, the development of e-banking and international payment services like Connect 24, ATMs, e-accounts, credit cards, SWIFT and the improved legislation of the banking sector. For example, before 2011, foreign banks had some restrictions on providing banking and financial services in Vietnam. From January 2011, however, and in compliance with World Trade Organization (WTO) commitments, foreign banks have been granted equal treatment as domestic banks in providing diversified banking and financial services, including deposits and lending, payment services, leasing, foreign exchange services and brokerage, use of derivative tools, asset management and financial consulting and information services. The next step was the introduction and application of international banking principles and standards (e.g., risk analysis and management, foreign exchange, loan classification and provisioning, accounting and auditing) (Nguyễn, 2007). In addition, the country's entry into international trade and investment agreements, such as the US-Vietnam Bilateral Trade Agreement in 2001 and its accession to the WTO in 2007, increased competitive pressure on the banking industry. In order to boost commercial banks' competitiveness, the government promulgated Decree 141 in 2006, which increased capital levels for all credit institutions. Accordingly, commercial banks are required to have at least VND3 trillion (USD143 million) in capital, up from the prior minimum of VND70 billion (USD3.3 million). Banks that did not meet this requirement by December 2010 would be forced to undertake merger and acquisition activities or to have their respective banking licenses revoked. As a result, a number of small rural banks transformed into urban commercial banks with a significant expansion in their total assets. There were also three newly established commercial banks (LienVietPostBank, TPBank and BaoViet Bank), while three banks (Vietcmbank, Asia Commercial Bank and Sacombank) went for a public listing on the stock exchange. Most of the remaining currently active banks tried to upgrade their scale and operations.

However, this rapid expansion in both the size and diversity of the banking system resulted in structural weaknesses. Since 2008, suffering from the spillover effect of the GFC, Vietnam experienced macroeconomic instability with high inflation and an economic slowdown, and the banking system showed tensions and vulnerabilities, such as accelerating credit and liquidity risks, worsening performance and competitiveness, complex shareholding structures and inadequate corporate governance. In 2011, the SBV decided to conduct a comprehensive restructuring scheme, with aggressive actions to address the high level of NPLs, widespread cross-ownership and other structural problems in order to enhance the efficiency and productivity of the banking sector. Weak banks have been forced to either merge with other banks or be taken over by SBV for nothing. At the same time, the regulatory banking framework has been revised and converged to international standards. Domestic banks also face pressure to raise capital to comply with the requirements of Basel II.

With this brief background of the banking sectors of the seven economies under examination, we now present a literature review focussing on the increasing integration of financial systems across the countries, their repercussions and the studies that have analysed these international networks and the possible contagion that this integration entails.

## 4 Literature Overview

There has been an extensive number of empirical research studies that analyse potential systemic crises and contagion risk using VNA, which has become a well-recognized tool for mapping potential risk within the financial system. The key advantage of this approach is that financial linkages can be mapped on a truly global scale. A number of studies have been published by central banks, financial regulators, practitioners and academics that focus on the factors that may trigger contagion risk. In particular, special attention has been given to the issues of systemic risk, intra- and cross-border contagion risk and the role of SIBs. These studies unambiguously show the vulnerability of systemic banking stability to the transmission of shocks – see, for example, Allen and Gale (2000), Haldane and May (2011), Minoiu and Reyes (2013), Yellen (2013), Cerutti (2015) and Yilmaz (2017), among others.

Recent empirical studies on the GFC indicate that high capital inflows to emerging market and developing economies can be traced back to excessive global liquidity. This excess liquidity provided cheap US dollars, while at the same time forcing global investors to seek higher yields and returns by shifting their portfolios towards emerging markets with higher interest rates and better economic prospects. As a consequence, we witnessed excessive capital flows to emerging markets, developing economies and less-developed economies. Anecdotal evidence thus confirms that high and unstable capital flows undermine financial stability.

Cihak and Ong (2007) examined the scope for cross-border spillovers among major EU banks and found that spillovers were more likely to happen within domestic banking systems, but that cross-border links were expanding more than the domestic banks, which evidently supported the need for strong cross-border supervision. One important funding source was parent-bank lending during and after the crisis, especially when other funding sources were not available. By the early stage of the GFC in 2007, domestic savings were significantly reduced and there was a widening funding gap. As Cihak and Ong (2007) argued, during the GFC, these funding gaps widened further due to the depreciation of domestic currencies that increased the weight of foreign-exchange loans in the stock of credit, lifting debt burdens of borrowers even more (Cihak and Ong, 2007). Therefore, parent-bank lending accounted for a significant and increasing share of financing of these funding gaps in many countries. The growth in foreign currency lending was mainly to borrowers in the private sector who did not hedge, which resulted in a build-up in vulnerabilities during the run-up to the crisis. The main risks leading to financial stability were an insufficient domestic funding base, deteriorating quality of banks' assets and increased exposure to the property market (Cihak and Ong, 2007).

Battiston et al. (2016) argued that because the global financial system has become increasingly large and interconnected, which is a key factor in precipitating a financial crisis, as trouble in one financial institution spreads quickly to others. They used a network analysis to explore the financial sector as a complex system of interlinked agents, where they assessed the likelihood of systemic contagion, the different channels through which contagion can spread, the linkages between the network and the resilience of the financial system. A further study by Benelli et al. (2011) explored cross-border financial linkages and identified key driving factors and the complexity that aided instability in the global financial system. The network showed that financial linkages had become more complex, with advanced economies still dominating the network of links across asset classes and regions, both as sources and recipients. Emerging markets then showed the strongest links with advanced economies, although linkages among the emerging economies increased rapidly during the last decade as well.

Upper (2007) mapped out how the links in interbank trading across borders can stimulate a credit default or liquidity contraction on the banks. Nier et al. (2008) showed how the transmission of market and idiosyncratic shocks can be simulated, which becomes important for identifying the triggers of contagion risk from market or idiosyncratic shocks. That helps one assess the impact of risk-sharing on cross-border interbank activities, which addresses solvency and liquidity contagion risks and also ensures effective prudential management policies by regulators.

A common theme in the literature on cross-border finance is that the majority of global financial flows is intermediated by a number of large and complex financial institutions (LCFIs) that operate in a small set of countries, serving as global common lenders and borrowers. The resulting transactions with LCFIs as counterparties comprise the core of cross-border financial flows and connect countries with one another (IMF, 2010).

The transmission of external shocks channelled by interest rates, exchange rates and other developments that form part of transactions with these counterparties threatens the stability of the financial system. The shocks so channelled work their way into the domestic financial system via cross-border financing intermediated mostly by banks. It is in this regard that Smaga (2014) underscored the inherent vulnerability of banks to contagion. A contagion effect is attributed to understating the increased systemic risk or negative externalities caused by cross-border activities and interconnectedness. However, for systemic contagion to occur, the institution from which the distress originates must be systemically important to affect other institutions and the financial system as a whole. Once (systemically important) sources of distress are identified, it is important to consider the potential shock transmissions and exposures to vulnerabilities that the banking sector could face. Peltonen et al. (2015) provide a discussion on how the transmitted shocks pass through both domestic and cross-border interconnections.

There are domestic economic conditions that interact with cross-border shocks absorbed by the domestic financial system. The study of Ahrend and Goujard (2012), for instance, underscores the role that strict financial regulations play in lessening contagion risks. One of the main findings of the study is that countries with a less-leveraged banking sector and a lower credit-to-deposits ratio face a lower risk of bank-balance-sheet-driven contagion that could lead to a banking crisis. In addition, increased external debt has caused domestic credit expansions, boosting the likelihood of a banking crisis. These analyses corroborate earlier OECD findings (Ahrend et al., 2011) that indicators of regulatory and supervisory strength are correlated with how well countries escaped damage to their banking sector during the GFC. While stricter financial oversight reduces overall financial fragility, there are some indications that stricter domestic banking supervision may increase short-term foreign bank borrowings due to regulatory arbitrage or increased attractiveness on the part of financial investors, which could further expose the banking sector to balance-sheet shocks.

Ahrend and Goujard (2011) and Ahrend and Schwellnus (2012) further suggest that countries with stronger banking supervision are less affected by investor-sentiment-driven capital flow reversals and thus have a lower risk of suffering from financial crises. Overall, lower risks and less vulnerability to international bank balance-sheet shocks could be achieved by longer debt maturity, better-capitalized banking systems and adequate central bank reactions during financial turmoil (Ahrend and Goujard, 2012).

## 4.1 Contagion Risk in Financial Markets

Prior to a discussion of contagion risk and bank cross-border interconnectedness, it is important to look at how the term *systemic risk* is established and positioned within the economic literature that deals with contagion risk. Undoubtedly, the term *systemic risk* is broadly applied, and its definition varies. We adopt the definition that is used by the Group of Ten (G10, 2001, p. 126):

> Systemic financial risk is the risk that an event will trigger a loss of economic value or confidence in, and attendant increases in uncertainty about, a substantial portion of the financial system that is serious enough to quite probably have significant adverse effects on the real economy.
>
> Systemic risk events can be sudden and unexpected, or the likelihood of their occurrence can build up through time in the absence of appropriate policy responses. The adverse real economic effects from systemic problems are generally seen as arising from disruptions to the payment system, to credit

flows, and from the destruction of asset values. Two related assumptions underlie this definition. First, economic shocks may become systemic because of the existence of negative externalities associated with severe disruptions in the financial system. If there were no spillover effects, or negative externalities, there would be, arguably, no role for public policy.

Gerlach (2009) showed that this definition provides three key factors that capture important characteristics of systemic risk. First, it must impact a 'substantial portion' of the financial system. Thus, it is the risk to the financial system as a whole. Second, systemic risk has multiple spillover effects (i.e., a single bank facing severe financial distress can undermine the financial stability and soundness of other banks that are connected to it). Such a situation requires that the effects of this risk are somehow measured and the potential impact is quantified, if possible. It is important to mention that systemic risk could be triggered by adverse macroeconomic conditions as well.

Degryse and Nguyễn (2004) provided an additional way of detecting potential triggers of interbank contagion risk. They use the following three fundamental explanations. First, interbank contagion attains its momentum in the case of insufficient financial liquidity for a specific financial market. They correctly underscore the fact that domestic and cross-border interbank markets provide liquidity only through the redistribution channel, which on its own fails to create new financial assets (liquidity). It is commonly observed from a number of financial crises that the key element that causes a liquidity crisis is the fact that an individual bank, or even the entire banking system, relies too heavily on the liquidity provided within domestic or cross-border markets. This can also be a reflection of the adopted business model by the bank in question. A further factor that often causes a liquidity constraint occurs when banks suddenly change their exposure to the interbank market due to their own liquidity problems or business activities. It is important to note that withdrawal from the interbank market is a much easier and cheaper option for a bank than the liquidation of its long-term position. Hoggarth et al. (2010) showed that large international banks respond to a liquidity problem by reducing their exposure to the interbank market, rather than reshuffling their liquidity across their branches and subsidiaries.

The next factor that can contribute to systemic turbulence within the banking system is a change in market expectations. This can cause contagion and have spillover effects across the entire market and/or the cross-border interbank market. Such a situation occurred during the Asian Financial Crisis in 1997, for example, when banks faced unprecedented asset-liability mismatches. The latter became even more pronounced when the currencies of those countries depreciated, which led to runs on banks in some countries. The interbank market almost froze overnight, aggravating the problem. Finally, the third way in which systemic contagion can occur is through the failure of SIBs. The failure of a SIB not only may cause a systemic crisis of the banking system in the specific country, but an ensuing spillover effect can be contagious for the banking systems of neighbouring countries. The degree of contagion depends on the linkages across banks through domestic (cross-border) interbank markets. The main area of concern here for our purposes is, therefore, the evaluation of the linkages of those SIBs within the domestic and cross-border interbank markets that are key players in terms of both liquidity provision and asset activities.

The increasing connectedness among the financial systems of different countries with each other is one of the most prominent features of globalization. The opening of capital accounts in developing economies contributed to this rising integration (Agenor, 2013). As discussed in Agenor (2013), international financial integration can benefit countries through multiple potential channels via smoothing of consumption through international risk sharing, improvement in domestic investment and growth, increased discipline at the macroeconomic level and increased efficiency and stability of the domestic financial system. However, this integration does not come without associated costs. With the increased globalization and integration of financial channels across countries, the risk of contagion spreading from a shock in one country to another connected country has only been rising. In fact, it has been argued that these networks can contribute to the amplification of financial booms and boost, which in turn causes crises (Borio and Disyatat, 2011; Borio, 2014), making them not only a factor for the spread of the crisis but also the reason for the crisis in the first place. Borio et al. (2014) found that the international monetary and financial system raises the risk of financial crises, which have significant macroeconomics costs. In fact, Dungey and Gajurel (2015) argued that the crises that are transmitted across borders are difficult to tackle by domestic policymakers alone. Cerutti et al. (2014) also discussed the fact that global financial linkages and the channels spreading spillovers have become increasingly complex. Tonzer (2015) argued that international banking, which can have positive effects during periods of stability, should be treated cautiously during periods of turmoil, as they may affect the entire network. The GFC of 2007–2008 and its aftermath have once again brought these issues to the fore. There is also evidence that those emerging economies that had direct or indirect exposure to banks in crisis-affected countries experienced higher capital outflows during the crisis of 2007 (Park and Shin, (2017). This shows that banking integration can also have an impact on other sectors of the financial system as well.

## 4.2 Network Models: Theoretical Concepts

A seminal paper by Allen and Gale (2000) derived a contagion model within a financial market equilibrium framework, where financial contagion is modelled as an equilibrium phenomenon. They show that because liquidity preference shocks are imperfectly correlated across regions, financial institutions hold precautionary claims on other regional financial institutions. Such a mechanism is perceived to reduce risk against liquidity preference shocks. Allen and Gale (2000) further argue that the key factor that triggers contagion across the financial institutions (markets) is determined by the structure of the claims within the financial market system. It is then evident that systemic changes within the financial (banking) market can affect systemic changes within both the core-periphery and the core-core network. The authors further show that such interconnectedness can have a positive effect on the efficient allocation of financial funds by improving financial innovation and competition.

There is prevailing empirical support that a well-developed global financial network contributes to accelerated economic growth. Anecdotal evidence indicates that economic growth in emerging and less-developed economies depends significantly on bank lending. Undoubtedly, competitive pressures within a global network of financial institutions can have a favourable effect on how capital is allocated. At the same time, a number of financial (banking) crises demonstrate that the network across global and multinational financial (banking) institutions undermines the stability of an individual banking system through adverse contagion risk. The latter occurs through systemic instability within the banking system and financial institutions. Glasserman and Young (2015) show that strongly interconnected financial systems report higher losses caused by contagion risk. The threat of contagion risk has multidimensional effects on emerging and less-developed economies that have rather limited economic stabilizers to withstand the adverse effects of contagion risk, which can be escalated via cross-border interbank activities. Glasserman and Young (2015) further show that this is reinforced even more strongly in cases where bank activities are linked through off-balance-sheet financial activities. In this regard, possible turbulences in terms of lending disruptions involving quite complex cross-border interbank linkages may contribute to a spillover effect for other financial institutions.

There have been studies that have tried to identify the relative importance of these channels in the crises of the recent past. OECD (2012) highlighted the role of cross-border banking contagion in the GFC of 2007–2008 and mentioned that bank balance-sheet contagion can be of a direct nature through 'lending-country spillovers' and indirect banking contagion through 'common-creditor contagion'.

It further discussed that crisis risk has been bigger for common-creditor contagion. Forbes (2012) discussed that shocks arising in one country in the form of increases in stressed assets and a lowering of bank deposits can spread to other countries because of the resulting reduction in bank credit in those other countries to restore capital adequacy.

Frexias et al. (2000) model systemic risk in an interbank market. Their research question explores how the banking system is capable of withstanding the insolvency of one bank. They also explore whether or not the closure of one bank could cause a knock-on effect on the rest of the system. An integral part of their model is the investigation of how the central bank can coordinate to avoid the negative consequences on the payment system, including the doctrine of TBTF. Mirroring Allan and Gale (2000), Leitner (2005) also argues that an interconnectedness of financial institutions improves the allocation of scarce resources through innovation and competitiveness. He shows that interconnectedness across banks is beneficial if it can push banks in a crisis to provide financial support for one another (bailing them out). This effect is, however, subject to their ability to coordinate such events. Gai and Kapadia (2010) argue that models with endogenous network formation, such as Leitner (2005), impose strong assumptions. They also state that the existing literature fails to differentiate between the probability of contagious default and the potential way it is propagated. Gai and Kapadia (2010) expanded existing analytical models of contagion in financial networks by allowing an arbitrary structure. In particular, they assessed two key channels of contagion in financial systems through which default may spread from one institution to another. The primary focus is on how losses can potentially spread via a complex network of direct counterparty exposures, following an initial default. They argue that the probability of contagion is generally low, but that the effect, once contagion occurs, tends to be widespread.

## 4.3 Counterfactual Simulations[13]

While network analysis has aided our understanding of the risks posed by greater interconnectedness, actual occurrences of default cascade events (referring to instances of a bank's default impacting or inducing default of other banks via direct balance sheet linkages or indirect linkages, such as precipitation of bank runs following a loss of confidence) remained rare even during the height of the GFC, largely due to widespread regulatory intervention. This has led to the lack of reliable empirical evidence, which allows for reasonably accurate estimation of such risks and their impact on the financial system and economy

---

[13] This section is based on Sababathy and Ling (2019).

upon the materialization of such events. Against this backdrop, counterfactual simulations have emerged as an important approach to assess the likelihood of contagion occurring (Upper, 2011; Elsinger et al., 2012). Such simulations are increasingly being used by regulators, either on a stand-alone basis to assess the resilience of a particular financial system or as part of a broader macroeconomic stress testing approaches, as in the case of the Bank of England's RAMSI model (Burrows et al., 2012).

Upper (2011) reviewed counterfactual simulation studies of bank-driven contagion, specifically via the interbank market channel, and found two major shortcomings in the extant literature. The first was an exaggerated focus on the idiosyncratic failure of an individual bank in constructing shock scenarios. The second was the general neglect of mechanisms that extend beyond direct balance-sheet linkages. Such mechanisms, like the amplification of losses by agents' behaviour and asset pricing, which can be significant during crisis periods, can lead to a misleading conclusion that contagion risk is small.

The early literature on counterfactual simulations that takes into consideration interbank exposures established two premises. First, it appeared that the contagion of insolvency due to interbank exposures is rare. Second, it is difficult to create realistic scenarios that will induce a significant amount of contagion (Summer, 2013). The more recent literature, however, has emphasized the importance of considering other contagion channels in constructing counterfactual simulations. Glasserman and Young (2015) highlighted the importance of mechanisms that go beyond simple spillover effects (referring to the default cascade approaches) to magnify shocks, such as (i) bankruptcy costs and (ii) valuation losses resulting from a deterioration of counterparty creditworthiness or a loss of confidence. In particular, they found that a loss of confidence can lead to widespread losses in value – with their analysis suggesting that this channel of contagion is likely to be more important than simple spillover effects.

Put differently, a possible explanation for the general neglect of other forms of contagion mechanisms could have been the reliance on default cascades to propagate distress within networks (i.e., distress within the network is only induced upon the failure of a bank in response to either a common shock or idiosyncratic events, a rather common feature across early counterfactual simulation; Upper, 2011; Elsinger et al., 2012; Glasserman and Young, 2015). Beyond being an unrealistic assumption in light of how recent financial crises events have unfolded, the default cascade approach turned out to be problematic for another reason: it is difficult to induce contagion conditional on bank defaults, limiting the usefulness of such simulation studies. For example, given banks are typically subjected to single counterparty exposure limits that generally fall well below banks' total capital, a simulation study with a shock scenario involving a single defaulting bank would neither be sufficient to cause other banks' default nor induce widespread contagion. To stimulate meaningful contagion in such studies, one has to create a shock scenario with simultaneous instances of bank defaults within the financial system, which are both rare and, again, unrealistic in actuality.

The DebtRank measure, which was motivated by work on the concept of distance to default and enabled the propagation of distress within a network without assuming defaults (Battiston et al., 2012), gained prominence as a method to estimate the impact of shocks within financial networks (Aoyama et al., 2013; Tabak et al., 2013; Bardoscia et al., 2015; Fink et al., 2016; Bardoscia et al., 2017). Of significance, the DebtRank measure that uses the relative loss of bank equity within a network as a measure of distress allowed for both the propagation of distress induced by valuation losses within networks following the deterioration of counterparty creditworthiness or a loss of confidence to be incorporated in simulation studies. Consistent with this, the impact of shocks measured using DebtRank is typically larger than the traditional default cascade approach, given the ability to induce further losses within the network. Battiston et al. (2016), who inaugurated the DebtRank measure to carry out a stress-test exercise on interbank exposures of 183 listed European banks over the years 2008–2013, found that the second- and third-round effects of distress dominate first-round effects, further underscoring the importance of taking into account other contagion channels/mechanisms in counterfactual simulation. The original DebtRank measure assumed that distress, and thus losses, were propagated linearly between connected banks. This assumption was subsequently relaxed in later studies (Bardoscia et al., 2016; Bardoscia et al., 2017) to introduce other non-linear propagation functions.

## 4.4 An Overview of Empirical Research in Network Analyses

The empirical research on interbank linkages and contagion risk is rather voluminous. Representative studies include Sheldon and Maurer (1998), Furfine (1999) and Wells (2002). While Boss et al. (2004) focus on case studies in European countries, Upper and Worms (2004) analyse contagion risk in the United States. Undoubtedly, they help policymakers better understand the complexity of the financial network, although they fall short on providing general policy recommendations and policy actions needed to deal with an eventual manifestation of contagion risk. A further notable study involving VNA was published by Nier et al. (2007). The study is underpinned by the seminal paper by Allen and Gale (2000). However, Nier et al. (2007) provide much deeper insights into the area of contagion risk by exploring possible financial contagion effects. They show that banks that are well capitalized compared to their peers are more resilient against possible contagious effects. They also show that a relatively marginal change in bank connectivity can trigger disproportional contagion effects. At the same time, if connectivity reaches a threshold value, bank connectivity can help banks that are mutually connected to withstand possible shocks. Nier et al. (2007) also find that the size of interbank liabilities can have a negative impact on bank stability through domino effects. That can occur despite sufficient capital reserves. In terms of competition, they provide evidence that a higher degree of concentration within the banking system can trigger larger systemic risk.

Hattori and Suda (2007) explored the 'core-periphery' network of cross-border bank exposures for 215 countries using the BIS's Locational Banking Statistics data for the period from 1985 to 2006. They found that the network has become more tightly connected with a higher average degree, higher clustering coefficient and shorter average path length over time. In addition, network features remain largely undisrupted by any of the disturbances or crises in international financial markets. Although a systemic risk build-up is inevitable over time, financial markets are allocating capital and risk more efficiently.

Minoiu and Reyes (2013) provided a comprehensive analysis of the global banking network using data on cross-border banking flows for 184 countries over the period from 1978 to 2010. They showed that the density of the global banking network was pro-cyclical. They also provided interesting evidence that country connectedness increased before financial crises and dropped afterwards. In the paper, they further argued that the network density in 2007 was comparable to earlier peaks. Minoiu and Reyes (2013) posited that network density tends to expand and contract in line with the cycle in capital flows. Furthermore, country centrality decreased during and after banking and sovereign debt crises, with the GFC standing out as an unusually large disruption to the global banking network, contradictory to the findings in Hattori and Suda (2007). A more recent study by Korniyenko et al. (2018) further explored the global financial network.

Utilizing data on bilateral cross-border exposures between 1980 to 2005 for eighteen advanced and emerging economies, Kubelec and Sa (2010) found increasing financial interconnectivity over time. The global financial network was clustered among a few key nodes with large financial links and lower average path length over time, focusing on the United States and the United Kingdom as the central hubs. Due to its robust, yet fragile, network structure, disturbances to the key hubs would transmit shocks rapidly and widely throughout the network. Comparison with the trade network showed similar increases in interconnectivity over time. Nonetheless, the trade network exhibited strong intracontinental links, concentrating around three clusters, a European cluster (centred on Germany), an American cluster (centred on the United States) and an Asian cluster (centred on China).

There are a number of studies that included India in their cross-border banking network and contagion analysis. Dungey and Gajurel (2015), in their study of banking contagion in fifty-four countries during the period from 2007 to 2009, employed a capital asset pricing style framework and found that India exhibited all three channels of contagion via systematic, idiosyncratic and volatility shocks. However, only idiosyncratic shocks increased the likelihood of systemic crisis in the country. Minoiu and Reyes (2013) used network analysis on confidential location-based flow data provided by the BIS and defined a global banking network with a core–periphery structure. They found that in the run-up to the crisis of 2008, the BRIC countries (Brazil, Russia, India and China) were among the most integrated borrowers alongside countries of emerging Europe. The Reserve Bank of India also conducts network and contagion analysis in its half-yearly Financial Stability Reports at a national level to identify both the dominant banks in the sector and the dominant sectors in the overall financial system.

## 5 Data and Methodology

### 5.1 Data Description

As Fender and McGuire (2010) argued, the GFC demonstrated that the type of available information that would be needed by regulators to identify international funding risks is inadequate. Along the same lines, Cerutti et al. (2012) pointed out that data quality was an important issue in the analysis of systemic risk. Finally, McGuire and Wooldridge (2005) reviewed the currently available data sources for research on contagion effects and systemic risk. As highlighted in McGuire and Wooldridge (2005), the BIS currently provides three types of statistics on international banking activity: Locational Banking Statistics (LBS), Consolidated Banking Statistics (CBS) and Syndicated Loan Statistics (SLS). LBS provides information on the external debt measures that use national accounts or the balance of payments. LBS are generally used by national statistical offices for the construction and evaluation of the balance of payments statistics, while CBS and SLS contain information regarding cross-border borrowing sourced from individual banks.

It is important at this stage to point out the differences of how the data are reported. McGuire and Wooldridge (2005) provide a detailed explanation of how these two sets of statistics differ from conventionally applied measures of external debt. The locational statistics cover cross-border positions of all banks domiciled in the reporting area, including positions vis-à vis their foreign affiliates. But the consolidated statistics report the nationality of the reporting bank as well as their net out intragroup positions (McGuire and Wooldridge, 2005). Minoiu and Reyes (2013) advocate the use of LBS as the most appropriate statistics if the aim is to explore linkages across countries.

The focus of our analysis is to capture and subsequently explore the global financial network structure as it pertains to the Asia-Pacific region. The LBS data set is available from the BIS for this purpose. We should note that LBS data are unconsolidated, which means the data sample includes positions vis-à-vis affiliates of foreign banks that reside in different countries. We only use data on loans and deposits on banks' balance sheets.

The sample period runs from 1998 Q1 to 2018 Q1 for nine core countries (Australia, Canada, France, Germany, Japan, Luxembourg, Switzerland, the United Kingdom and the United States). Six other economies (namely Hong Kong, Italy, Macau, South Korea, Taiwan and the Philippines) started reporting their banking flow statistics to the BIS after 1998. Therefore, the number of core and periphery countries varies over time.

The different types of claims on reporting economies include loans and investments to counterparty economies (borrowers). Liabilities of a reporting economy include deposits and borrowings from counterparty economies (lenders). As we may observe from Figure 1, both total claims and liabilities increased over time, reaching a peak in 2008 Q1 before plummeting during the financial crisis. Cross-border banking flows have gradually recovered since 2009 Q1. We find similar trends for total claims and liabilities of the G7 countries, Switzerland and Luxembourg. However, they exhibit different development after the GFC. Both total claims and liabilities stagnated and have not yet recovered to their pre-crisis level.

Figure 2a provides a comparison of the volume of cross-border flows by taking into consideration the full network and contrasting it with Figure 2b, which shows the flows when bilateral transactions between the G7 countries, Luxembourg and Switzerland are excluded.

## 5.2 Network Settings

Our sample includes major economies in the Asia-Pacific region and other globally systemically important economies. In total, we collected data for twenty-eight economies. We have nine global core countries (the G7 countries as well as Switzerland and Luxembourg), six regional core economies (AU, HK, TW, KR, MO, PH) and the remaining thirteen countries have been

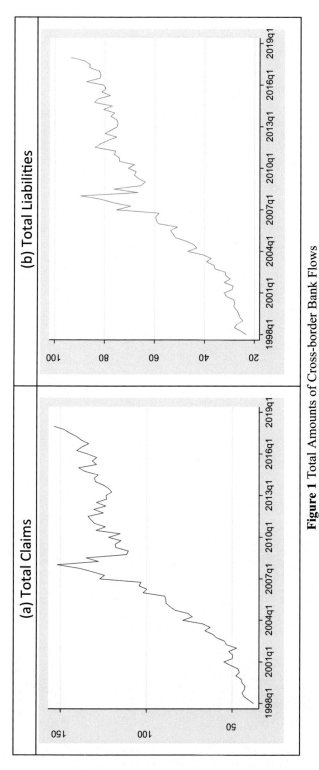

**Figure 1** Total Amounts of Cross-border Bank Flows

**Notes:** Total claims (liabilities) is the sum of all cross-border banking claims (liabilities) between reporting and counterparty countries. The data is modified using the exchange rate and break adjusted changes based on BIS calculation. Total claims and liabilities are in 100 billion USD.

**Source:** BIS Locational Banking Statistics.

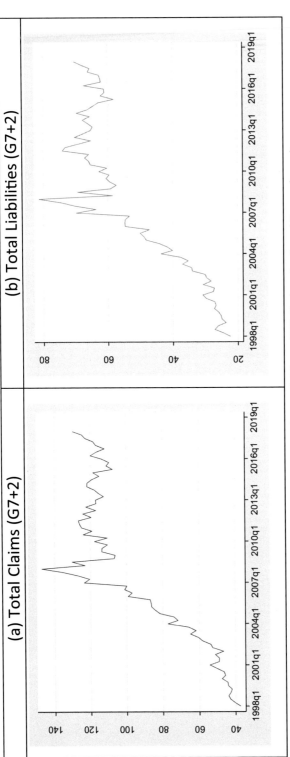

**Figure 2** Total Amounts of Cross-border Bank Flows (G7, Switzerland, and Luxembourg)

**Notes:** Total claims (liabilities) is the sum of all cross-border banking claims (liabilities) between reporting (only G7 countries, Switzerland, and Luxembourg) and counterparty countries. The data is modified using the exchange rate and break adjusted changes based on BIS calculation. Total claims and liabilities are in 100 billion USD.

**Source:** BIS Locational Banking Statistics.

designated as periphery economies (BD, CN, IN, ID, MY, MM, NP, NZ, PK, SG, LK, TH, VN).[14] Core economies are defined as reporting economies to the BIS' Locational Banking Statistics. As mentioned previously, the available data set imposes certain restrictions that have to be taken into consideration. We need to map the network structure of core economies. However, some economies do not report these data, so these are treated as periphery economies.

As Chan-Lau et al. (2007) showed, by using the network simulation approach, we may assess direct and indirect cross-border interbank contagion risk caused by liquidity and/or solvency problems. In order to establish cross-country interbank linkages, we have to project a matrix that captures the exposures of individual banks. Working with central banks would allow us to collect data on bilateral exposures that provide a more detailed understanding of the potential contagion risks.

Our network consists of a set of nodes that are represented by the 28 economies in our sample. Thus, each node represents an individual economy. A link to another economy then represents financial claims on the total banking system in that economy. The proposed network is constructed as follows: economies are represented by nodes and edges capture the flows of money. The orientation of links runs from source to target economies. Our network structure is a directed network that includes both in-coming and out-going links. Specifically, the evidence based on the links from sources to targets provides valuable information about which economy holds claims (liabilities) of other economies (through nodes). In our network structure, some nodes (economies) are positioned as a source but also as a target of bank flows. Other nodes (economies) represent a target only.

The individual linkages contain numerical values that capture the volume of claims (liabilities) across the entire network. The weights of edges represent the number of bank flows for each edge. In our VNA, we can also define the size of nodes, the colour of nodes and the thickness of arrows to reflect different network features. The pattern and size of linkages in our VNA contain a wealth of information and provide a comprehensive picture that may help to fully understand the complexity of the captured linkages. The resulting structure also allows us to identify the key economies that dominate the system in terms of the flows of money to periphery economies.

## 5.3 Network Measurements: Applied Indicators

The next part of our discussion focuses on the fundamental network indicators that are vital for our analysis.

---

[14] See Table A3 in the Appendix for the complete list of economies and their abbreviations.

The *node degree* provides fundamental information about the number of links associated with a given node. As Kolaczyk (2009) explains, we can easily calculate the number of incoming (in-degree) and outgoing links (out-degree) in a directed network structure. In other words, in-degree captures claims and out-degree captures liabilities. The concept of node degree indicates the number of edges connected to a node (economy). An economy with a high node degree has a large number of cross-banking contracts among the region. For a directed network, in-degree can be defined as the number of bilateral links to a target economy, while out-degree refers to those from a source (reporting) economy. We can further obtain information about the total amount of cross-border flows by using the *weighted node degree (node strength)*, giving rise to the weighted out-degree and/or weighted in-degree for a given node (economy). The latter two capture the intensity of financial flows for a particular economy (node). We should note that in our network, out-degree and weighted out-degree for periphery economies, is equal to zero. We may interpret the node degree as follows: a higher node degree refers to the number of bilateral cross-border bank transactions. In the case of the complete network, a decrease in weighted out-degree reflects reduced bilateral transactions among advanced countries.

A further important network indicator is *connectivity*, which is measured by the ratio of the total number of links (edges) that exist in the network to the number of total possible links (edges). In other words, connectivity measures network density, or, alternatively, it can be interpreted as the likelihood of a connection between two economies (Minoiu and Reyes, 2013).

*Betweenness centrality* is a measure for the relative frequency of a node appearing in the shortest paths between every other pair of nodes in the network. This measure is intended to show the place of a node in the network and reflects how influential an economy is as an intermediary of flows in the network. A higher centrality value of an individual node (economy) indicates a higher importance of an economy in the network. This measure captures the transmission of contagion effects: nodes with higher centrality values have a larger influence on other nodes (economies).

The betweenness centrality for node $v$ is computed as follows:

$$BC(v) = \sum_{s,t \in N} \frac{\sigma_{s,t}(v)}{\sigma_{s,t}}$$

where $\sigma_{s,t}$ is the total number of the shortest paths between node $s$ and node $t$, $\sigma_{s,t}(v)$ is the number of the shortest paths between $s$ and $t$ that contain node $v$. The betweenness centrality reflects how influential a country is as an intermediary of money flows in the network.

Two additional summary statistics include *closeness centrality* and *eccentricity*. The former is defined as the average distance from a given starting node to all other nodes in the network. Closeness centrality thus measures the mean distance from a node to other nodes. This quantity has a low value for nodes that are separated from others by only a short distance on average. Such nodes could have better access to information at other nodes or a more direct influence on other nodes. Newman (2010) shows that this indicator is a natural measure of centrality and is often used in social and other network studies. There is one issue with this indicator, related to the fact that its values tend to span a rather small dynamic range from largest to smallest. As Newman (2010) further shows, this problem has practical implications, because it is difficult to distinguish between central and less central nodes using this measure. The distance between two nodes can be defined as the length of the shortest path between them. Closeness centrality is the average distance from a given starting node to all other nodes in the network. In particular, closeness centrality is computed as the reciprocal of the sum of the distance between a given node and all others:[15]

$$C(v) = \sum_{s \in N} \frac{1}{d(s,v)}$$

where $d(s, v)$ is the distance between the nodes, $s$ and $v$. Therefore, the more central the node is in a network, the closer the node is to all other nodes.

The second summary statistic, *eccentricity*, measures the distance from a node to the farthest node from it. *Node strength* refers to the value of net interbank exposures originating or terminating at a given node. An increase in the amount of interbank lending by a creditor to its counterparties shows greater node out-strength. Although the number of outward links signals the importance of the bank as a credit provider in the system, the amount of lending should also be emphasized when determining the riskiness of the entity as a credit provider. To put it simply, a bank (*A*) that lends to a single entity with an amount of MYR100 million is riskier than a bank (*B*) that lends to five different counterparties with an amount of MYR20 million each. This paper adopts the weighted network approach proposed by Opsahl et al. (2010) by considering the total number of counterparties a bank lends to (out-degree) and the weighted size of exposures using a tuning parameter, $\alpha$. By assigning $\alpha = 0.5$, both the number of out-degree and weight of the links are given equal relative importance. This centrality measure enables us to more accurately assess the contagion risk of

---

[15] To compare the measure across different networks, closeness centrality can be normalized by multiplying the reciprocal by the number of all nodes, $N$.

banks with a high out-degree relative to the size of interbank placements with their respective counterparties

Fagiolo (2007) expands the standard clustering coefficient of Watts and Strogatz (1998) for unweighted and undirected networks to binary directed and weighted directed networks. Tabak et al. (2011) show in the case of the Brazilian banking system that the directed clustering coefficient is a suitable indicator for measuring systemic risk in complex networks. The *clustering coefficient* measures the completeness of a neighbouring node. In our analysis, we apply the binary clustering coefficient, the value for which ranges from 0 to 1. This coefficient is calculated as the ratio between the total number of complete triangles to the total possible number of such triangles.

## 6 Empirical Results

### 6.1 Cross-Border Activities in the Asia-Pacific Region

As illustrated in Genberg (2017), cross-border financial integration has become rather complex in Asian emerging market economies (AEME). Following many years of relatively high economic growth that was predominantly financed by banks, cross-border interbank linkages in the AEME now contain a strong global network component. We have witnessed a dramatic expansion of cross-border activities, predominantly in the form of cross-border bank lending. This acceleration of cross-border activities was driven particularly by international banks from the more advanced economies, including the G7 countries and both global as well as regional financial centres – Singapore, Hong Kong and Kuala Lumpur. Von Peter (2007) provided a detailed analysis of how international banking activity has changed since the 1990s. His analysis unambiguously showed that international lending activities were dominated by only a handful of global banks from advanced economies. For example, in 2016, the UK held 20.4 per cent of international bank assets and 22.8 per cent of international bank liabilities. With a share of 12.6 (9.2) per cent in terms of bank liabilities (assets), the United States constituted the second-largest financial centre. Japan, by contrast, has seen a contraction in terms of international lending activities, most likely on account of the long-standing banking restructuring process. It is also of interest to note that Japanese banks do not provide lending directly to less-developed economies, but rather allocate their assets to the financial centres in Hong Kong and Singapore. The other G7 countries, such as Germany and France (as well as Switzerland, which is not a G7 member), have significantly lowered their exposures to international lending activities to single-digit percentages.

The current global economic and political uncertainty could undermine the fragile stability in emerging and less-developed economies. In particular, the recent interest rate increases by the Federal Reserve, as well as the termination of quantitative easing in the United States and Europe, could put extra pressure on the financial liquidity position of financial institutions in Southeast-Asian economies. A resulting capital outflow combined with currency depreciation could have an adverse effect on systemic stability. The recent global outflow of funds from the emerging economies to the tune of USD12.3 billion has undermined the stability of domestic currencies. And a global economic slowdown could aggravate the situation even more. Furthermore, countries also face the problem of political and economic uncertainty. The current trade disputes between the United States and China could have adverse consequences for Asian economies as a whole. It is well documented that a reduction of China's exports could negatively affect supply chains across Southeast Asia, as regional trade with China is based on the trade of intermediate goods, which accounts for more than 50 per cent of overall trade. In terms of internal economic and political issues, many Southeast Asian economies exhibit a high share of household debt that is linked to aggressive competition among retail banks and non-financial institutions expanding their business activities into the retail banking sector.

On the other hand, countries are better equipped to withstand shocks coming from contagion effects. Asian-Pacific economies have put a lot of effort into the key factors that should alleviate potential contagion effect compared to the Asian financial crisis in 1998, including modifications of exchange-rate regimes. Many economies have abandoned the fixed currency pegs that prevented a devaluation of their currencies in the case of sudden financial market turbulence. That should prevent the sharp, crisis-led devaluations that we witnessed in 1998 when, for example, the Indonesian rupiah and the Malaysian ringgit depreciated by more than 75 and 50 per cent, respectively, against the US dollar. The current setting of the exchange rate regime, such as a managed float that Southeast Asian economies have consequently adopted, should considerably reduce the problem of sudden and rapid devaluations of their currencies.

A further important step that should significantly contribute to the reduction of possible contagion effects is the fact that most economies in the region have substantially boosted their foreign exchange reserves. In fact, some economies have increased their foreign exchange reserves tenfold since 1998. That should help protect them from short-term speculative attacks on their domestic currencies. Moreover, many economies have addressed the problematic aspects of fiscal deficits, and fiscal discipline has been documented in a number of emerging and less-developed economies in the region. This goes hand in hand with curbing inflationary pressures that might undermine overall financial and economic stability and cause unwanted contagion damage if financial market turbulences were to materialize.

## 6.2 Network Connectivity Measurements

We also try to capture the dynamics of lending relationships in the selected seven economies over the observed period. Such a detailed analysis will disclose the potential for partially hidden problems that might trigger a banking crisis through contagion effects.

Table 1 provides a basic overview of the various network indicators. We can see that the selected economies in our sample borrow from 7.3 lenders on average and up to 15 lenders in total. In each quarter, the borrowed volume is on average equal to USD54.4 billion, with a range from zero (minimum) to

**Table 1** Summary Statistics of Network Indicators

**Claims**

|  | Obs | Mean | SD | Min | Max |
|---|---|---|---|---|---|
| **Measures of country centrality** | | | | | |
| **Network excluding transactions among advanced economies** | | | | | |
| In-degree | 2268 | 7.308 | 3.697 | 0 | 15 |
| Weighted in-degree | 2268 | 54460.7 | 104178.5 | 0 | 934564.8 |
| Out-degree | 906 | 18.295 | 4.694 | 4 | 27 |
| Weighted out-degree | 906 | 136332.2 | 177590.3 | 709 | 1378037.0 |
| **Measures of network density** | | | | | |
| **Network excluding transactions among advanced economies** | | | | | |
| Connectivity | 81 | 0.659 | 0.031 | 0.595 | 0.719 |
| Clustering coefficient (all) | 81 | 0.366 | 0.132 | 0.064 | 0.480 |
| Clustering coefficient (reporting) | 81 | 0.216 | 0.087 | 0.050 | 0.352 |
| Betweenness | 81 | 8.967 | 1.287 | 6.867 | 12.667 |
| Closeness | 81 | 0.761 | 0.033 | 0.692 | 0.813 |

**Source:** Matousek (2019).

USD934 billion (maximum). Core economies lend on average to 18.3 economies, and the maximum number of economies that receive loans is 28. The
volume of flows in core economies ranges from USD0.79 billion to USD1,378
billion. The bottom panel of Table 1 provides information regarding network
density. We observe that the likelihood of two economies being connected
through cross-border flows falls into the interval from 59.5 to 71.9 per cent.
As for the binary clustering coefficient, we find that two economies having a
connection with one another, if they both have a relationship with a third
economy, is on average 36.0 per cent for all economies and 21.6 per cent for
reporting economies. *Betweenness centrality* (i.e., the relative frequency of a
node appearing in the shortest path between every other pair of nodes in the
network) is on average 8.96. The indicator of closeness centrality varies from
0.69 to 0.81.

Cross-banking contracts capture the changes in bilateral links to a target
economy. We observe that the average number of links to target economies
increased steadily since the early 2000s. Over this period, we observe several
significant adjustments in terms of the quantity of bilateral cross-border activities, which may reflect structural changes after the dot-com bubble and the
period before the GFC. However, a significant change can be seen shortly after
the peak of the GFC. The number of cross-border in-coming links has increased
from 2013 Q2 and has continued to grow. We observe that the volume of cross-
border lending has increased consistently over the entire period, which is
reflected in node strength, capturing the total flows. In addition, we find a
structural break shortly after the GFC in 2008.

By contrast, cross-border links from source to target economies display a
steady pattern with a brief drop during the period of the GFC. The strength of
the nodes, however, increased from the relatively low values observed in 1998
and reached USD1,137 billion shortly after the GFC.

In order to provide information about cross-border banking transactions in
selected Asia-Pacific economies, we plot two panels in Figure 3. Figure 3a
shows the strength of nodes for our full network. We observe that there has been
a clear drop in the volume of cross-border activities shortly after 2007, which
most likely reflects credit contractions faced by individual financial systems,
predominantly in the United States and Europe. However, Figure 3b demonstrates that once we exclude the bilateral links within the G7 countries,
Luxembourg and Switzerland, regional economies in Asia have not been significantly affected by the crisis. We can see a gradual growth in terms of the
volume of bank loans, with only a partial adjustment shortly after the GFC.
Nevertheless, this fall was reversed very quickly. We may argue that financial
markets in advanced economies have shifted to emerging markets and

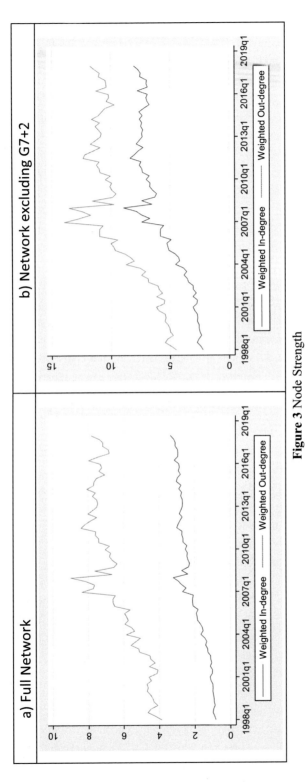

**Figure 3** Node Strength

**Notes:** The unit of cross-border banking transactions is 100 billion USD.

**Source:** Matousek et al. (2019).

less-developed economies as a consequence of the increased uncertainty in the United States, Unite Kingdom and the rest of Europe. We might also speculate whether QE could have contributed to the increased liquidity in those economies. So far, the evidence of empirical research studies is rather inconclusive. A more intuitive explanation and discussion is provided by visual network graphs below.

In Figure 4, we turn our attention to the clustering coefficient. As we have discussed earlier, the clustering coefficient is a possible indicator for providing valuable information about systemic risk in complex networks. From Figure 4b, we observe a structural change in the early 2000s, when the value of the coefficient jumped up over the subsequent periods, indicating a higher probability that two economies are connected through a third economy. In other words, increased values of the coefficient indicate that there has been a tendency for higher clustering in the network over the period. Since we observe that increase from early 2000 (i.e., before the GFC), we may surmise that there has been a tendency for the financial markets to create regional clusters and that financial markets have become more connected.

We can further explore the issue of how the network is mutually linked or connected by using the network connectivity coefficient. Let us recall that connectivity measures network density. If we focus just on Figure 5a, we observe that the coefficient has increased over the analysed period, which suggests that cross-border activities within the region have increased. This lends support to our earlier conclusions based on changes in the clustering coefficient.

In Figure 6, we look at the closeness centrality network coefficient. We again provide two panels – that is, the full network and the full network without the bilateral links of the G7 countries, Luxembourg and Switzerland. There is strong evidence that the coefficient that measures closeness dropped sharply at the outset of the GFC. We can observe a similar sharp decrease in 2000–2001 during the dot-com crisis. While Figure 7b provides a similar pattern, the drop in the coefficient values over the period is less pronounced than in Figure 7a. By contrast, we find an increasing trend. We recall that low values for nodes that are separated from others by only a short geodesic distance on average indicate that such nodes may have better access to information at other nodes or more direct influence on other nodes. Thus, the low value of the coefficient indicates that the distance of individual (economy) node has increased, which can be interpreted as large financial centres playing a key role in the network. However, Newman (2010) argues that there is a problem with this practical implication since it is difficult to distinguish between central and less central nodes using this measure.

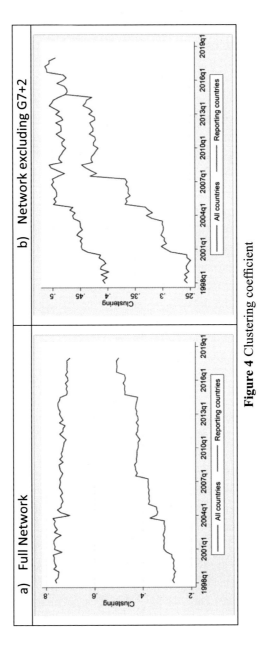

**Figure 4** Clustering coefficient

**Source:** Matousek et al. (2019).

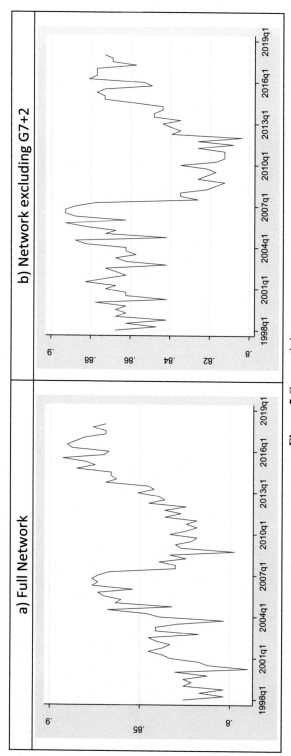

**Figure 5** Connectivity

**Source:** Matousek et al. (2019).

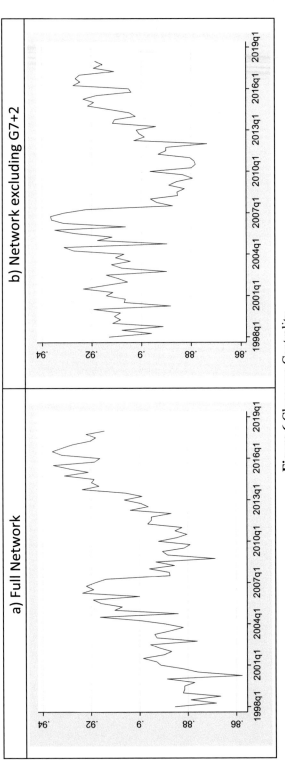

**Figure 6** Closeness Centrality

**Source:** Matousek et al. (2019).

Finally, the last network coefficient is betweenness centrality, which provides information about the influence of an individual economy as an intermediary of flows in the network. A closer look at Figure 7 indicates that coefficient values have gradually declined. This corresponds to our previous discussion that the system has become more clustered and none of the economies were able to maintain a dominant position within the market compared to the period of the late 1990s and early 2000s. We can further observe some degree of volatility of the coefficient during the GFC, but since 2010 there has been a clear tendency of a diminishing role for a few key players. This outcome will also be observable in the network graphs that we discuss later. This trend is further supported by Figure 8, which focuses on the influence of advanced economies (G7, Luxembourg and Switzerland) on the regional network only. Based on the presented figures, we conclude that financial markets have been undergoing substantial changes that were further reinforced or amplified by the GFC.

## 6.3 Visual Network Analysis[16]

In this section, we extend our discussion by providing a visual presentation of network analysis. We plot network graphs for claims and liability data using the Gephi software.[17] In order to highlight bank flows in the Asia-Pacific region, bilateral transactions between advanced economies (G7, Luxembourg and Switzerland) are excluded in the network graphs. This is because the amount of bank flows among these advanced economies tends to be much larger than the amount of flows between advanced and other Asia-Pacific countries or among the Asia-Pacific countries.

Three features of the figures – the size of nodes, the colour of the nodes and the thickness of edges – can represent different aspects of a network structure. In the following network graphs, the node size indicates the weighted out-degree, the colour of a node indicates betweenness connectivity and the thickness of arrows indicates the number of bank flows.

Finally, we present the ranking of network measures by focusing on in- and out-weighted summary statistics.

Figure A1 provides a detailed analysis of how the flows of money have changed during the entire period. It highlights the complete picture of bank flows in the Asia-Pacific region, including bilateral transactions between advanced economies (G7, Luxembourg and Switzerland). In addition, Figure A1 provides information about the weighted out-degree, which is represented by the size of a node. The colour of nodes indicates the betweenness centrality

---

[16] This Section is based on the results that were prepared by Seohyun Lee.

[17] Gephi is an open-source visualization software for network graphs (https://gephi.org/).

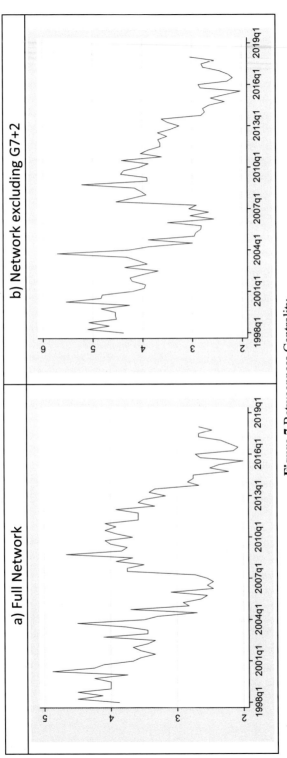

**Figure 7** Betweenness Centrality

coefficient and the size of bilateral bank flows is reflected in the thickness of the edges. We analyse each period from 1998 Q1 to 2018 Q1 and show graphs for the first quarter of selected years. What we can observe from Figure A1 is that, based on the betweenness centrality measure and the thickness of edges, the UK and Japan played a key role in terms of money flows over the period from 1998 to 2014. Since then, however, Hong Kong has taken the lead along with Japan and Australia, while the UK's dominance in the network has fallen significantly. South Korea also plays an important role in cross-border banking activities, while Taiwan's position in that market has remained more or less unchanged. The colour of nodes, which represent betweenness centrality, become brighter over time, reflecting the growing importance of economies like Taiwan, South Korea, Macau and China.

In Figure A2, we present measures of weighted in-degree (the size of nodes), betweenness centrality (the colour of nodes) and the size of bilateral bank flows (the thickness of the edges). This structure, however, has been gradually changing with the increasing position of Taiwan. In fact, by the second half of 2010 the regional economies had caught up. In 2018, we can see the important role of China (CA), South Korea (KR), Taiwan (TW) and Macau (MO), among other countries. We can also observe from 2014 onwards that a number of economies in the region have become more influential in terms of the betweenness centrality measure. These economies include, among others, Vietnam (VN), Myanmar (MM), Bangladesh (BD), India (IN) and Thailand (TH).

The changes in the importance of individual economies find further support in Table 2, which shows the ranking in terms of both the weighted out-degree and weighted in-degree measure. We readily observe some changes in terms of the full network, primarily for China and Hong Kong. Table 3 reports the changes in terms of the regional network when G7 and Switzerland and Luxemburg are excluded.

## 6.4 Assessment of the Philippine Banking System's Cross-Border Exposures[18]

The increasing trend in cross-border lending exposes banks to distress, uncertainties and even burden-sharing during a crisis. When banks respond to a deterioration in their balance sheets through reductions in cross-border loans, financial contagion in the international banking system could be triggered. For instance, during the recent crisis, several Central and Eastern European banks that were particularly exposed to Western European banks suffered a

---

[18] This Section is based on the empirical findings provided by Dizon et al. (2019).

**Table 2** Top 10 Countries Based on the Node Centrality Measures

| | 1998 Q1 | 2000 Q1 | 2007 Q1 | 2008 Q1 | 2009 Q1 | 2010 Q1 | 2012 Q1 | 2016 Q1 | 2018 Q1 |
|---|---|---|---|---|---|---|---|---|---|
| **Weighted in-degree** | US | US | GB | GB | US | US | US | US | US |
| | GB | GB | US | US | GB | GB | GB | GB | GB |
| | DE | DE | FR | FR | DE | FR | DE | FR | FR |
| | IT | IT | DE | DE | FR | DE | FR | JP | JP |
| | FR | CH | CH | IT | IT | IT | JP | DE | DE |
| | JP | FR | IT | LU | LU | LU | LU | LU | CN |
| | SG | JP | LU | CH | CH | JP | IT | CN | LU |
| | LU | LU | JP | JP | JP | CH | CH | IT | SG |
| | CH | SG | CA | CA | CA | CA | SG | SG | CH |
| | CA | CA | SG | SG | SG | SG | CA | CA | IT |
| **Weighted out-degree** | GB | GB | GB | GB | GB | GB | GB | GB | GB |
| | JP | JP | DE | DE | US | US | JP | JP | JP |
| | FR | CH | FR | US | JP | JP | US | US | FR |
| | DE | DE | US | JP | DE | FR | FR | FR | US |
| | CH | US | JP | FR | FR | DE | DE | DE | DE |
| | LU | FR | CH | CH | LU | LU | LU | HK | HK |
| | US | LU | LU | LU | CH | CH | CH | LU | CH |
| | AU | AU | AU | CA | CA | CA | AU | AU | LU |
| | | | TW | AU | AU | AU | CA | CH | CA |
| | | | KR | TW | TW | TW | TW | CA | AU |

Table 3 a) Ranking of Regional Network Measures (Weighted Out-Degrees)

| 1998 | 2000 | 2002 | 2004 | 2006 | 2008 | 2010 | 2012 | 2014 | 2016 | 2018 |
|------|------|------|------|------|------|------|------|------|------|------|
| SG | SG | SG | SG | SG | SG | SG | SG | CN | CN | CN |
| HK | AU | AU | AU | AU | AU | AU | AU | SG | SG | SG |
| KR | KR | KR | KR | HK | KR | HK | CN | HK | GB | HK |
| AU | HK | HK | HK | CN | HK | CN | HK | AU | AU | AU |
| CN | CN | US | US | US | CN | KR | GB | GB | HK | GB |
| TH | TH | CN | CN | KR | US | US | US | KR | US | US |
| ID | ID | NZ | TW | GB | GB | GB | KR | IN | JP | JP |
| IN | IN | IN | GB | TW | IN | IN | IN | US | KR | KR |
| MY | NZ | ID | NZ | IN | TW | NZ | NZ | TW | IN | IN |
| US | GB | TW | IN | NZ | NZ | LU | LU | LU | TW | TW |

Table 3 (cont.)

b) Ranking of Regional Network Measures (Weighted In-Degrees)

| 1998 | 2000 | 2002 | 2004 | 2006 | 2008 | 2010 | 2012 | 2014 | 2016 | 2018 |
|------|------|------|------|------|------|------|------|------|------|------|
| JP | JP | JP | GB | GB | GB | GB | GB | GB | HK | HK |
| GB | GB | GB | JP | JP | JP | JP | JP | JP | AU | JP |
| FR | DE | TW | AU | AU | AU | AU | AU | US | JP | AU |
| US | US | DE | US | TW | TW | US | TW | TW | TW | GB |
| DE | AU | US | TW | US | DE | TW | US | AU | GB | TW |
| AU | FR | AU | DE | DE | FR | FR | FR | FR | US | US |
| LU | LU | FR | FR | KR | US | DE | DE | DE | FR | FR |
| CH | CH | LU | LU | FR | KR | KR | KR | KR | KR | KR |
| IN | PH | CH | CH | LU | LU | CH | MO | MO | DE | DE |
| IT | CA | SG | MO | CH | CH | LU | LU | CH | MO | MO |

deterioration in their financial conditions as the latter tried to cut their exposure to the former in reaction to losses incurred in their asset portfolio.

Using the gross cross-border financial position of U/KBs and their subsidiary thrift banks and the quantity of cross-border exposure, Dizon et al. (2019) observe that there is an increasing trend of cross-border exposures (in terms of asset holdings) in the PBS, albeit at a gradual pace. In Table 4, we report the gross cross-border financial position, cross-border financial claims and cross-border financial liabilities. We observe that the gross cross-border financial positions grew by 17.1 per cent from USD40.1 billion as of end-March 2015 to USD46.9 billion as of end-March 2018.

Table 4 further shows that the Philippine U/KBs in total remain a net cross-border lender with a net cross-border financial asset position of USD8.9 billion as of end-March 2018. Meanwhile, year-on-year growth of cross-border exposures has averaged at 6.7 per cent. In terms of levels, U/KBs cross-border exposures relative to total banking system assets stood at 16.9 per cent as of end-March 2018.

Dizon et al. (2019) also showed that the majority of U/KBs' cross-border claims were from Asia Pacific economies, followed by claims from North American and European economies. In particular, Asia Pacific economies own a significant share in universal PDBs and government banks, and in commercial PDBs and FBBs. Likewise, the United States and Canada, which comprise the North American region, have sizeable shares in universal banks and in commercial PDBs.

In Figures A1 and A2, we may observe the cross-border positions of selected Asia-Pacific countries, including AU, CA, HK, JP, UK and US. The size of the 'nodes' represents the level of cross-border exposure of a particular bank category. The larger the nodes, the bigger is the said cross-border exposure (cross-border financial claims and liabilities) of a particular bank category. Meanwhile, the thickness of the 'edges' represents the magnitude of Philippine banks' exposure to a specific country. The thicker the edge, the more exposed a particular bank category is to a specific country. In terms of cross-border claims, the majority are claims to the United States, while the major sources of cross-border funding as of end-March 2018 are the United States and Singapore.

## 6.5 South Korean Cross-Border Activities

Based on the definition of the various network metrics, we compute these measures and analyse the trends of network measures for total claims and liabilities respectively. Lee (2019) shows that the number of out-links are larger

**Table 4** Cross-Border Exposures of U/KBs and Its Subsidiary TBs (in US$ Billion)

| Total cross-border claims | | | Total cross-border liabilities | | | Gross cross-border financial position[1] | | | Net cross-border financial position[2] | | |
|---|---|---|---|---|---|---|---|---|---|---|---|
| Mar-15[3] | Mar-18 | % change | Mar-15[3] | Mar-18 | % change | Mar-15[3] | Mar-18 | % change | Mar-15[3] | Mar-18 | % change |
| 21.9 | 27.9 | 27.7% | 18.2 | 19.0 | 4.3% | 40.1 | 46.9 | 17.0% | 3.6 | 8.9 | 144.8% |

[1] Sum of cross-border financial claims and cross-border financial liabilities

[2] Cross-border financial claims less cross-border financial liabilities.

[3] Data available as of end-March 2015.

**Source:** BSP-SDC, Dizon et al. (2019).

than that of in-links for South Korea. The in-degree represents the number of out-links from the reporting countries to South Korea among the entire sample countries. The average out-degree slightly increased after 2013, implying that Korean banks' asset holdings became more diversified in terms of the destination of loans.

Furthermore, Lee (2019) illustrates the development of the weighted in- and out-degree of South Korean cross-border bank flows. The level of the weighted in-degree is higher than that of the weighted out-degree, indicating that the amount of bank loans to South Korea is larger than the amount that Korean banks lend to other countries in the network. This is because the network includes advanced countries which South Korea relies on for funding. The weighted in-degree plummeted immediately after the GFC but gradually recovered after 2009. While there was a strong increase in the weighted in-degree in 2015, it flattened out afterwards. The weighted out-degree has shown a steady increase, implying the expansion of cross-border lending of South Korean banks.

The clustering coefficient for South Korea that we do not report here has risen substantially after 2015. As Lee (2019) argues, this implies that the countries neighbouring Korea became more interconnected within the network. Betweenness centrality also shows how influential South Korea is in the network. It increased during the GFC periods, suggesting that Korea played an important role in providing funding to the region as the other advanced economies were severely hit by the crisis. However, betweenness centrality has steadily fallen since 2011 as the troubled advanced countries recovered and the financial intermediation function that Korea had served during the crisis weakened. The indicator of closeness centrality decreased during the GFC period and recovered its level approximately after 2013 on average. Lee (2019) argues that this indicates that South Korea became closer to each node of the network as a lender and thus more central to the network. This is consistent with the previous finding that emphasizes the increasing role of South Korea as a funding source in cross-border banking flows network.

In the following discussion, we examine the network measures for total liabilities. With liabilities data, an out-link from South Korea means that Korean banks (borrowers) have deposits from non-residents (lenders). Analogous to this, an incoming link from a country to South Korea implies that Koreans (lenders) have deposit at foreign banks (borrowers).

As Lee (2019) shows, similar to the claims result, the out-degree clearly exceeds the in-degree, meaning that the number of countries to which Korean banks owe liabilities is larger than the number of countries which owe liabilities to Korean depositors. Over time, both the in- and out-degree have increased slightly, suggesting that the liability side of bank flows has become more diversified.

The level of the weighted out degree is much higher than that of the weighted in-degree. This implies that the amount of deposits from non-residents into Korean banks is larger than the amount of residents' deposits into the rest of the countries. In the first half of 2007, both the weighted in- and out-degree rose steeply. This may reflect improved financial integration in the regional banking sector. However, it seems that the GFC discouraged the development of financial integration. There were strong signs of retrenchments (a decrease in residents' deposit in foreign banks) and stops (a decrease in non-residents' deposit in Korean banks) during the crisis period.

Lee (2019) shows that after the financial crisis, the weighted out-degree levelled off while the weighted in-degree increased substantially starting in 2014. This increase in the weighted in-degree was mainly due to the entrance of Hong Kong's bilateral banking flows data from the 2014 Q4. In addition, an increase in Korean residents' deposits into US banks is one of the crucial reasons for the trend. Since US monetary policy normalization, markets have had a strong expectation of hikes in interest rates and appreciation of the US dollar. This expectation provides a motive for searching for higher yields that led to such an increase in deposits in US banks.

The trends in the clustering coefficient and betweenness centrality are somewhat similar to that of the claims data. Both graphs provide evidence of a highly connected regional financial network. As the network becomes denser, financially neighbouring countries of South Korea are becoming more interlinked and Korea's influence as an intermediary of banking flows has grown less significant.

For the period from 1998 to 2004, South Korea was not reporting the LBS data to the BIS. Thus, Korea is considered as a periphery country which receives funding from foreign banks and does not lend to the rest of the world. As shown in Figures A1 and A2, it borrowed from only eight advanced economies: the United States, the United Kingdom, Japan, Germany, France, Luxembourg, Switzerland and Australia. There was a structural change in the banking network in 2013 Q1. While the foreign claims held by Korean banks showed a robust increase, Korean banks held more assets of China (the share of Chinese assets in total foreign assets of Korea is 41 per cent) and Indonesia (4 per cent). In contrast, the proportion of claims of the United States (20 per cent) and the United Kingdom (5 per cent) declined. This implies that Korea became an important source of funding in the Asia-Pacific region. In terms of claims of Korea held by foreign banks, Japan, the United Kingdom and the United States are the main sources of Korean banks' funding.

In 2015 Q1, we observe that Hong Kong appears as a major player in the network. This is because Hong Kong had started to report the LBS data since 2014 Q4. In addition, it may be affected by the launch of the Shanghai-Hong Kong Stock Connect in November 2014. The Stock Connect allows mainland Chinese investors to purchase equities that are listed in Hong Kong and lets foreigners buy mainland Chinese stocks in a less restrictive manner. In consequence, it opened investment opportunities in China for a wider set of investors.

Major borrowers of Korean banks include China (the proportion of its assets owned by Korean banks out of total foreign assets amounts to 44 per cent), the United States (17 per cent), Indonesia (5 per cent), Singapore (5 per cent) and Vietnam (5 per cent). Countries with high Korean asset holdings are Hong Kong, Japan, the United States and the United Kingdom.

In 2018 Q1, Hong Kong remains an important funding source of the region. The network has become denser and more complex. Korean banks hold more US assets as the Fed has been normalizing its policy rate.

As for the liabilities network structure, we summarize only some key features here (see the network Figures A1 and A2 in the Appendix). From the network graphs from 1998 to 2004, we find that Korean residents had deposits in the banks of advanced economies, such as the United States, the United Kingdom and Japan. In 2005 Q1, South Korea started to report bilateral cross-border banking flows data to the BIS and both betweenness centrality and the weighted out-degree increased. However, Korea had no links with some less-developed countries, like Sri Lanka and Nepal. The liabilities of Korean banks were distributed mainly in the United States, the UK, China and Singapore as of the first quarter of 2018.

## 6.6 Cross-Border Activities in Indonesia

As Muhajir et al. (2019) show, Indonesia's cross-border interbank money market has experienced a negative impact after the GFC. In 2007 and 2008, we can observe that there was a squeeze in the cross-border interbank money market. In Graphs A1 and A2, we can see that according to the density derived from the many arrows in 2007, there were many linkages in cross-border interbank money markets. By 2008, however, the density had become lower compared to 2006. But the earlier trend was fully restored after 2010. Due to the confidentiality of systemically important banks in Indonesia, we disguise bank names/codes. We denote the types of banks as follows: SOB (state-owned bank), PLB (private-local bank) and FBB (foreign-branch bank). This confidentiality serves to help avert misperceptions about systemic banks, which should be perceived as banks that have a bigger cushion in order to be more resilient than non-systemic banks. The international banks, which are related within the cross-border interbank money market in Indonesia, have the status of global systematically important banks (G-SIB). The list released annually by the Financial Stability Board can be accessed publicly. The decision of whether a bank is systemic or not is made by the Financial Services Authority of Indonesia (OJK) and Bank Indonesia. The review is made twice a year to monitor and evaluate the existence of D-SIBs and to impose a capital surcharge on each bank.

Moving on, Muhajir et al. (2019) report that there are thirty banks that are mainly categorized as systemic banks in Indonesia. These systemic Indonesian banks dominate the market. Regarding the interconnectedness score, the three large banks yield a significant result on account of the high number of claims and liabilities in the intra-financial system. The number of linkages is not presented in this calculation but will be visualized when we run the network visualization below.

Identifying D-SIBs is essential because, in the case of Indonesia, there are 115 commercial banks, which may have a relationship through the cross-border interbank market; therefore focusing on D-SIBs will make this analysis more relevant since the D-SIBs essentially represent the Indonesian banking system. We found that not all the D-SIB banks are involved in cross-border interbank money markets. The position of Indonesia in cross-border activities can then be observed in Figures A1 and A2.

To better assess the Indonesian banking system and its connections, Muhajir et al. (2019) apply a network shock simulation following an approach introduced by Espinosa-Vega and Sole (2010). They project three shock scenarios, which were determined entirely arbitrarily and do not refer to an actual condition that can be derived with a macroeconomic credit-risk model. In the first scenario, the shock to the system is a credit shock, which represents a default of a bank's loan in the interbank money market. It highlights the loss resulting from one or more banks defaulting on their debt obligations. The first scenario is modelled on a default of a banking system's debt to other banks and how this default would hypothetically affect other banks in the network. The scenario given is that a bank's loss given default (LGD = $\lambda$) is 50 per cent. It is assumed that banks can roll over their funding sources and do not need to resort to fire sales of their assets.

The second scenario adds a funding shock to the credit shock that was imposed in the first scenario. In this case, institutions are unable to replace the funding previously granted by the defaulted institutions. While the LGD was 50 per cent in the first scenario, in the second scenario we are imposing a LGD of 100 per cent and the condition that banks are unable to recover the lost funding source(s) given to its borrower in the same exposure ($\rho$ = 100 per cent). It is still assumed that banks do not need to undertake fire sales of their assets.

The last scenario maintains the system's two previous shocks and adds a fire sale of assets set-up. The fire sales scenario means that banks are forced to sell their assets at a (severe) discount or a haircut scenario. This action is forced upon the banks because they need to roll-over their funding to meet their obligations. In the third scenario, the modelling approach sets LGD or $\lambda$ = 100 per cent and prescribes that banks are unable to recover the lost funding source(s), given to its borrower in the same exposure ($\rho$ = 100 per cent). In addition, banks face a haircut in terms of selling off their assets ($\delta$ = 75 per cent).

The results from the three scenarios in Muhajir et al. (2019) suggest that none of the banks in the system caused the failure of other banks. This outcome is supported by the fact that banks' capital in the system was adequate to mitigate the risks in the interbank markets. Nevertheless, they find that the capital level of the foreign bank group is relatively small compared to other bank groups, such as the state-owned and privately owned banks. This is also related to the fact that the foreign bank group is more active in the interbank money market than other bank groups. From these three scenarios, they also derive that there are no banks that are in a hazardous condition.

## 6.7 Cross-Border Activities in Papua New Guinea[19]

The foreign exchange interbank market is where banks trade different currencies to facilitate the trading of goods and services. An ideal interbank market ensures that there is competition for banks to buy and sell foreign exchange at a price that is fair to all dealers. The dealers can undertake foreign exchange deals for their clients or for themselves and are willing to offer prices to other participants as well as ask for prices. The foreign exchange interbank market in PNG has been dysfunctional, mainly from a lack of foreign exchange inflows since 2013, that resulted in an imbalance in the foreign exchange market. Aba (2019) argues that there is ample evidence for an imbalance in the demand for and supply of foreign exchange in the interbank market, where the demand for US dollar exceeded the supply of US dollar, leading to an oversupply of the local currency, spurred on by increased government spending that resulted in an increase in import orders. Aba (2019) explains that the key reasons for the shortage in foreign exchange were the fall in the prices of PNG's export commodities since 2011 and the end of the construction phase of the PNG liquefied natural gas (LNG) project in mid-2014, combined with some rigidity in the exchange rate, which did not adjust fast enough to accommodate the fall

---

[19] This Section is drawn from the information provided in Aba (2019).

in foreign exchange inflows into the economy. Given the inflexibility in the exchange rate, the role of the foreign exchange interbank market to set the price failed, resulting in the local currency (kina) not adjusting to find its equilibrium level. With the lack of foreign exchange interbank trading and no alternative markets to access foreign exchange, dealers that have a short position have no incentive to bid the kina exchange rate down. One of the main reasons why there is a bottleneck in the foreign exchange inflows is because only a small fraction of the export receipts is being repatriated back to PNG. In fact, project development agreements allow export proceeds to be held in offshore accounts.

Foreign exchange interbank trading is very critical in any economy, as it facilitates international trade and ensures that external balance is achieved. In the foreign exchange interbank market, the demand for and supply of foreign exchange should interact to determine the price (kina exchange rate) and meet the needs of both importers and exporters. Since 2012, the foreign exchange interbank market in PNG has not been functioning as a normal market would otherwise do. Aba (2019) lists four factors that caused the foreign exchange interbank market to not work. First, there was an absence of foreign exchange interbank transactions since mid-2012 to determine the value of the kina, which is an indication of the failure of the price-setting role of the foreign exchange interbank market. This caused an imbalance in the supply and demand for foreign exchange. Second, foreign exchange dealers were unable to meet the demand for foreign exchange and resorted to selling kina in the interbank market, while controlling the foreign exchange they provided to their clients. Third, the control of foreign exchange by dealers delayed resident firms from obtaining the foreign currency they needed to pay for their imports. It also meant that a few firms took a little longer in sending dividend payments abroad. Finally, there were some suggestions that the real effective exchange rate was overvalued compared to its equilibrium level – hence the need for flexibility and adjustment. A dysfunctional foreign exchange interbank market can limit the movement of capital between countries, especially making repatriation of profits and dividends difficult.

After 2011, the interbank foreign exchange market was a one-sided market where the local currency was flooding the domestic foreign exchange market on the back of a shortage in foreign currencies, especially the US dollar. To support their foreign exchange needs, domestic banks resorted to borrowing from their counterparties abroad or accessed the foreign exchange supplied by the central bank through its interventions to support the market. On an average basis, the holdings of foreign assets constituted around 7.9 per cent of total assets, while liabilities constituted 7.0 per cent of total liabilities. Both foreign exchange assets and liabilities declined over the period from 2010 to 2017. In Figure 8, we

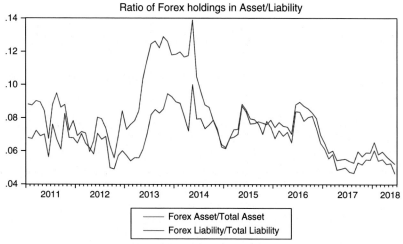

**Figure 8** Forex Holding of Banks

**Source:** Bank of PNG.

observe that after 2013, foreign exchange liabilities have matched foreign assets and continued to remain above foreign exchange assets, reflecting the shortage of US dollars in the domestic foreign exchange interbank market. This indicated that domestic banks had been borrowing foreign exchange from their counterparties abroad to meet their foreign exchange needs. This increase in foreign exchange liabilities could pose a threat to domestic banks if the shortage in foreign exchange is not addressed by the government.

As Aba (2019) shows, between 2005 Q4 and 2018 Q2, the network expanded with the inclusion of five new countries in terms of foreign liabilities, while it increased by three countries for foreign claims. Interbank trading by banks in PNG is limited to just banks within PNG and, to some extent, Australia. The other claims and liabilities relate to non-banking activities, especially in derivative contracts, extended guarantees and credit commitments. The expansion in the foreign claims network resulted from increases in PNG-registered companies' investments in France, Switzerland, Taiwan and Hong Kong, apart from their traditional investment destinations of Australia, Japan, Germany and Korea. This has somewhat increased the foreign exposure of PNG, and the likelihood of contagion spreading quickly to PNG through such a well-connected network.

PNG claims (foreign liabilities to PNG) increased from USD296.0 million in 2005 Q4 to USD307.541 million in 2018 Q2. We note that countries traditionally linked to PNG are Australia, Japan, the UK and Korea. The increase in PNG claims reflected the liberalization of foreign exchange controls, which gave PNG-registered foreign companies, especially mineral and petroleum companies, permission to use the project development agreements to invest their earnings in financial markets abroad. Combined with the higher price of commodities, the firms diversified their investments that led to an expansion in the network to include other countries such as France, China, the United States, Taiwan, Hong Kong and Switzerland. Australian-based banks have the largest share of 41.2 per cent in liabilities.

Foreign claims on PNG expanded to USD913.0 million from USD540.0 million. This reflected the expansion in the size of the networks as PNG attracted FDI from other countries, apart from its traditional lender countries, Australia and Japan. PNG has become one of the new frontiers for investments in mining and petroleum projects from the United States, France, Taiwan, Korea, Hong Kong and Japan. Most of the expansion in the financial network happened in 2008 and thereafter, directly related to the financing of the Exxon Mobile-led PNG LNG project, which commenced construction in 2008, the construction of the Ramu nickel/cobalt mine in 2012 and other mineral and petroleum investments in the country. The other factor included the liberalization of PNG's foreign exchange controls in 2005–2006, which paved the way for the flow of funds. Figure 12 below shows the network of PNG liabilities over the period from 2005 Q4 to 2018 Q2.

Japan and Australia both have assets worth over 10 per cent, while China has 4.4 per cent, Hong Kong has 6.4 per cent, France has 1.3 per cent and Korea has 2.3 per cent.

Figure 8 shows the claims and liabilities with respect to banking location from 2005 Q2 to 2018 Q2. From the chart, we can deduce that PNG's largest exposure occurred between 2008 Q2 and 2014 Q2. This is the period when the financing and construction of the PNG LNG project started and ended and FDI flowed into the country.

According to the cross-border position by banking location, Japan and Australia have the highest deposits in the PNG non-banking sector, while only Australia has the highest liability, both in the banking and non-banking sector. This indicates Australia's increased interest and dominance in the banking and non-banking sectors in PNG. There is also growing interest from Hong Kong and Taiwan.

## 6.8 Network Analysis in Malaysia[20]

In this Section, we analyse the trends in network measures for total claims and liabilities within the Malaysian banking system. The interconnectivity of banks experienced a relatively steep decline in 2015, before reaching 18.2 per cent in

---

[20] This Section is based on Sababathy and Ling (2019).

2017, compared to 20.7 per cent in 2013. As the number of nodes in the data set is fixed, the decline in connectivity is a factor of the total number of links in the network, which dropped to an average of 559 for the year 2017 from 627 in 2013. A further breakdown shows that this is largely attributable to fewer connections from SIBs, mainly made up by domestic players. The average number of transactions made by these domestic SIBs fell to an average of 281 in 2017.

As Sababathy and Ling (2019) show, the likelihood that two neighbouring counterparties are connected is also on a declining trend, with the clustering coefficient estimated at 14.8 per cent in 2017. There are generally two bouts of decline observed during the period, which occurred in 2014 and 2018. This is largely due to outflows, particularly to LIBFC. The results here signal that although fewer links are generated within the interbank market over time, the network is prone to the movement of flows, as shown by an increase in the intensity of cross-border flows.

Furthermore, Sababathy and Ling (2019) demonstrate that the change in betweenness centrality from 2013 to 2017 confirms that the role of some key SIBs remains important, recording a betweenness centrality of 0.05 to 0.08 as at 2017 Q4. The four largest parent SIBs remained as key financial intermediaries in the domestic market despite the declining role of their subsidiaries. Among the list of banks with the ten highest betweenness centrality statistic, two of the banks were LIFBCs, consistent with the significance of foreign players as a provider of foreign currency liquidity.

The average number of outgoing links has also been on a steadily declining trend, reflecting the decrease in the interconnectivity of banks (Sababathy and Ling, 2019). A fall in the average out-degree is observed since 2014 Q3. Focusing on the domestic interbank market only (the core-core network), given that there are 54 banks, the maximum number of potential outgoing links in this study is $(54 \times 53)/2 = 1{,}431$. However, given that there are only 169 directed-out links in 2017, only 12 per cent of the potential links are utilized, identifying the domestic interbank system as an incomplete network. This is not much different from 2013, when there were 216 outgoing links, thus exploiting 15 per cent of the potential core-core network. A look at the core-periphery structure, however, shows a slightly more complete network, with 54 per cent of the potential outgoing links between banks and their respective external counterparty countries being utilised as at end-2017. Sababathy and Ling (2019) argue that these findings seem to be justifiable since the greater regionalization of domestic banks, deep and liquid financial market, coupled with strong economic performance, attracted a larger presence of foreign banks. They further show that the decline in the average out-degree is more apparent for SIBs, albeit remaining higher than non-SIBs. This is largely attributed to the increase in cross-border flows, where more than half of exposures are to non-residents.

Sababathy and Ling (2019) also provide a breakdown of net interbank exposures of SIBs to non-residents, which shows that the largest exposure of domestic onshore banks was to the Asian region, specifically LIBFC. Intragroup funding to LIBFC expanded in mid-2014, following the increase in foreign currency lending to corporations to support business activities during the period. The general decrease in cross-border exposures observed in 2016 Q3, however, is partly explained by some domestic banking groups' strategy of reducing reliance on overseas operations on parent funding, limiting external exposures.

Table 5 shows the top ten net exposures of D-SIBs to non-residents by country. Net interbank placements in LBIFC as of 2013 Q1 was recorded at MYR5.4 billion. However, this figure ballooned to MYR11.7 billion as at end-2017, showing the increasing role of LIBFC as a booking centre. Cross-border interbank claims continue to be concentrated within the Asian region, particularly in countries dominated by domestic banks' regional presence.

The time evolution of cross-border activities in Malaysia is recorded in Figures A1 and A2. There is a decline in network connectivity in the cross-border interbank market over time, suggesting a decline in the network's susceptibility to contagion events. The decline in interbank

**Table 5** SIBs: Top 10 Net Exposures by Countries (2013 Q1 vs. 2017 Q4)

| | 1Q 2013 | | 4Q 2017 | |
|---|---|---|---|---|
| **No** | **Country** | **Exposure (MYR. bil)** | **Country** | **Exposure (MYR. bil)** |
| 1 | US | 7.1 | Labuan | 11.7 |
| 2 | Labuan | 5.4 | Singapore | 3.1 |
| 3 | Hong Kong | 2.5 | US | 2.2 |
| 4 | Singapore | 2.2 | China | 1.6 |
| 5 | China | 1.2 | Philippines | 1.1 |
| 6 | Indonesia | 0.9 | Hong Kong | 0.8 |
| 7 | France | 0.8 | Indonesia | 0.6 |
| 8 | UK | 0.8 | Japan | 0.6 |
| 9 | Vietnam | 0.5 | UK | 0.5 |
| 10 | Philippines | 0.5 | Korea | 0.5 |

**Source:** Bank Negara Malaysia.

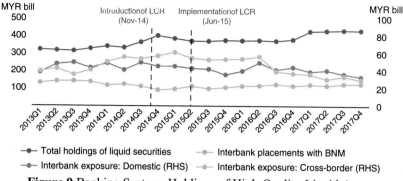

**Figure 9** Banking System: Holdings of High-Quality Liquid Assets
**Source:** Bank Negara Malaysia.

connectivity can be explained by the following: (i) greater cross-border flows to specific non-residents by SIBs and (ii) concentration of interbank activities with related counterparties (i.e. intragroup exposures) – a less risky source of exposure.

The LCR requirement, which was first announced in November 2014, could have contributed to the diminishing connectivity within the interbank network. To meet this requirement, banks are required to equip themselves with high-quality liquid assets (HQLA), which include placements with central banks and holdings of liquid debt securities. In this regard, banks would have been incentivized under the requirement to increase placements with BNM (i.e., lending to BNM in the domestic interbank market) as opposed to lending to another financial institution within the domestic interbank market as the former counts as a HQLA, thus lowering interconnectivity. Following the implementation of the LCR requirement in June 2015, Figure 9 does show a general decline in interbank lending by banks, while placements with BNM rose and remained at elevated levels thereafter.

## 6.9 Cross-Border Contagion: Evidence from Indian Banks[21]

The reforms in Indian banking in the post-liberalization era provided some impetus to the international operations of the Indian banks. However, the Indian banks operating cross-border are still subject to a number of regulations and restrictions. International banking transactions remain regulated under the overall partial capital account convertibility framework prevalent in India.

---

[21] This Section is based on Sharma (2019).

The top three countries of residence with the highest share in international liabilities are the United Arab Emirates (UAE), the United States and the United Kingdom. Many of these countries host significant parts of the Indian diaspora abroad and, hence, are a major source for non-resident Indian (NRI) deposits in India. In the case of consolidated international claims of banks on an immediate country risk basis, the highest proportion is that for the United States, followed by the UAE, Singapore, the United Kingdom and Hong Kong. While the United States and the United Kingdom are important international financial centres, Singapore and Hong Kong are important offshore financial centres. Hence, the risk materializing in these economies in general, and the banking sector in particular, may have potential spillover effects on India. Despite the increasing share of India in global cross-border banking activity, its share remains very low. This may be attributed to the regulations on borrowing and lending across borders. In fact, among the BRICS (Brazil, Russia, India, China and South Africa), the share of India is also not very significant. More specifically, the share of India in cross-border claims has been more or less the same for the period before, during and after the GFC of 2007–2008. Hence, in the context of the global international banking scenario, the role of India is limited.

Owing to the regulations on international banking activities in the country, Indian banking remained shielded during the international crises of the recent past. In general, Indian banks continued to operate normally in the aftermath of the GFC as outlined in Kumar and Vashisht (2009) and Sinha (2011). The main reasons cited for the normal functioning were the limited exposure of Indian banks to troubled assets, the prudential regulation by the regulator and a limited presence of foreign banks in India (Sinha, 2011). However, indirect effects of the crises still impacted Indian banks by putting pressure on domestic liquidity on the back of sudden reversals of foreign capital (Kumar and Vashisht, 2009). The Reserve Bank of India (RBI) took a number of measures to ease liquidity conditions to ensure normalcy (Sinha, 2011).

Cross-border banking in India remains somewhat muted. We first discuss the network analysis in the context of cross-border liabilities, followed by a discussion of cross-border claims. Among India's major counterparties in terms of cross-border liabilities, the United States, the United Kingdom, France, Germany and Japan are the most connected, as indicated by their weighted degrees. In the case of cross-country claims as well, the role of India is depicted in terms of ranks. However, the results of this data come with the caveat that the analysis has been done on a limited number of countries. In the analysis of the entire set of countries, the results may differ from the current results. Overall, countries like the United States, the United Kingdom, France, Germany and

Japan are among the most important players in the cross-border banking network pertaining to India.

In the context of the global cross-border banking scenario, the Indian banking sector's international operations are subject to regulations prescribed by the central bank in the purview of the existing legal framework under the overarching partial capital account convertibility. Most of the international operations of the banking sector in India are devoted to catering to the needs of NRIs, exporters and foreign currency credit needs of residents. Further, most of the international liabilities and claims are denominated in Indian rupees, lowering currency risks. The cross-border banking activities of banks operating in India are subject to prudential regulations that translate into lower exposures for these entities to cross-border risks. Further, the presence and operation of foreign banks in India are also limited. In this scenario, cross-border contagion risks remain limited for the country as seen by India's banking sector's experience in the wake of the international and regional financial crises of the recent past. The results from our observations and analysis using the BIS global data sets and the RBI's data also point towards the same and show that the role of India is not that significant in the global banking network. The results from the network analysis corroborate these findings, where the ranking of India in the network measures among the major countries with which it shares cross-border banking relations is not very high. The prudential approach of the country in terms of cross-border banking operations has shielded the banking sector from the effects of the crisis that originated in foreign countries.

## 6.10 Systematically Important Banks and Network Analysis: Evidence from Vietnam[22]

In the following Section, we try to shed light on bank's resilience in the Vietnamese banking system, where the latter is measured by the adequacy of the bank's capital and liquidity in case a particular bank faces shocks to the predefined risk factors. In other words, we perform a top-down stress test to assess the impact of D-SIBs on the performance of the banking system in Vietnam.

The data underlying the stress test consist of audited consolidated financial statements of fifteen banks identified as D-SIBs from 2017, as well as hypothetical scenarios based on real market and bank-system conditions in Vietnam, such as bad debts, the rate of cross-ownership, the exchange rate, interest rates and real estate prices.

---

[22] This Section is based on Nguyễn et al. (2019).

As Nguyễn et al. (2019) argue, D-SIBs in Vietnam are defined as credit institutions (CIs) and branches of foreign banks that have systemic importance. The latter is meant to signify that they have the ability to cause a negative impact on the entire system of credit institutions and foreign bank branches and/or when systemic risks disrupt the operation of the system of credit institutions, branches of foreign bank and the whole economy in case of insolvency. Using static quantitative indicators for identifying D-SIBs in Vietnam, the authors aim to provide a starting point for officially defining more stringent requirements for regulating and supervising CIs recognized in this category (D-SIBs) compared to other CIs in the future. The analysis also addresses structural systemic risks arising from CIs being TBTF and the 'orderly exit of small weak banks' that are not systemically important. Based on the current level of development of the Vietnamese banking sector, they provide simpler quantitative indicators compared to earlier empirical studies on Vietnam in the literature. However, their approach still maintains the suitability and reliability for identifying D-SIBs in Vietnam.

Nguyễn et al. (2019) assess the systematic importance of banks in two steps. First, they define quantitative scores using a set of indicators of scale, degree of alignment and substitutability. Second, the CIs use qualitative assessments and other monitoring information to supplement the quantitative assessment in the first step. Banks can be removed from or added to the list identified in the first step.

The systematic importance of the banks in the sample was assessed according to the index-based measurement method, based on the scores of the indicator groups: size, interconnectedness and substitutability:

i) *Size.* This is the primary measure of systemic importance. The larger the bank, the more likely it is that the sudden stop of a service will be widespread and therefore the more likely it will be for the bank to disrupt financial markets, the banking system and even the broader functioning of the economy. This measure looks at the overall size of banking activity in the system (or the economy) and provides a precise measure of the potential systemic impact in the event of a bank collapse.

ii) *Interconnectedness.* This indicator represents the degree of association of a bank with other financial institutions that may give rise to external factors affecting the financial system and the domestic economy in Vietnam. Systemic risk can occur through the insolvency of a bank that has a significant impact on the financial system.

iii) *Substitutability.* This indicator assesses the systemic importance of a banks in its operation as a provider of infrastructure services. The bigger the bank, the harder it is to replace it, and the more likely it is that the risk will cause a disruption in the event of a bank failure. The level of importance of a bank's systems increases, as other credit institutions are less likely to provide similar services in the event that the bank ceases to operate.

The SBV combines the results of the quantitative scores with the qualitative assessment coming from the results of the regular inspections and supervision of D-SIBs, taking into account the complexity of the bank, the number and size of branches, the number and size of subsidiaries, the level of complexity in the operation, derivative transactions and the role and importance of the financial infrastructure, which includes the role of the payment system.

For the group of 15 D-SIBs, borrowing and deposit-taking from the interbank market in 2017 was in relatively small amounts in proportion to the total assets of most of these banks. Contagion risks were assessed based on the interbank matrix which includes the net lending between banks in the system.

The model of Nguyễn et al. (2019) makes an implicit assumption about the effects of the default of an individual bank at some point on all of its interbank obligations and the impact on other banks. More specifically, if the default of a bank on its interbank obligations implies the default of another bank within the system, then a second iteration of the model should be undertaken to assess the impact of the bank default on all other banks.

Their results indicate that contagion risks are very low. In particular, the impact of a bank default on its interbank obligations from other banks will stop at the first iteration without the contagion of insolvency on other banks in the interbank system.

Finally, the authors also use the BIS's Locational Banking Statistics data, which cover individual countries and the amounts outstanding of cross-border bank exposures between Vietnam and other countries. The reporting countries are required to report the credit exposures of their domestic banks to other countries in the country list and the amount outstanding of credit exposure from each reporting country to the other countries. From the list of reporting countries, there are only twelve out of thirty-one countries with reporting data. Based on this available data, the authors assessed that there is no impact from the reporting countries on Vietnam.

Nguyễn et al. (2019) also observed that cross-border activities in Vietnam are rather restricted and that there were no substantial changes over time, as can be seen from Figures A1 and A2. These two figures provide a detailed analysis of how the flows of money have changed during the entire period. Figure A1 shows the weighted out-degree, which is represented by the size of a node. Figure A2 then presents measures of the weighted in-degree (the size of nodes), betweenness centrality (the colour of nodes) and the size of bilateral bank flows (the thickness of the edges). The figures do not reveal any significant changes in terms of the cross-border activities in Vietnam. Nevertheless, we observe that the betweenness centrality measure has become more important in Vietnam.

## 7 Conclusions and Policy Implications

This study provides a comprehensive analysis of the development in cross-border banking activities over the last twenty years. The analysis is based on the BIS' Locational Banking Statistics. In order to provide an overall picture of how banking systems are interconnected, we deploy VNA. We explain in great detail how this methodological framework can contribute to a better understanding of the issues under investigation. This technique clearly demonstrates not only the complexity of cross-border bank activities within the Asia-Pacific region but also its connectedness with advanced economies.

The data sample from 1998 to 2018 allows us to trace the structural changes that have occurred, particularly during the financial turbulences that took place in either the region or in the advanced economies. The analysis investigates the characteristics of cross-border activities in the Asia-Pacific region. Reported network summary statistics include measures such as closeness centrality, betweenness centrality, connectivity and clustering. The analysis of these coefficients over the sample period helps us better understand structural changes over time. We have also evaluated the role of individual economies in our network over time. Our network analysis shows that the volume of transactions has dramatically increased, particularly after 1997. This change was accompanied by an increased number of bilateral links across banks. We note that many of the peripheral economies have become increasingly influential in the overall network. We also show that the connectedness of economies in the Asia-Pacific region since 1997 has changed completely, specifically that the structure of how economies are connected now is significantly different. There is evidence that the links have become much closer and that the volume of credit transactions has increased severalfold.

Several key policy implications can be drawn from the analyses of financial networks. Although central banks and regulators in the region have implemented various regulatory measures to mitigate the systemic risks due to cross-border financial interconnectedness, there is still room for improvement. Authorities in the region need to be more cooperative. Sharing information between home and host countries is crucial for establishing the ground for multilateral cooperation in banking regulation. Constructive dialogue with banks is another way to support financial stability. It is important for policymakers to consider the balance between prudential objectives and efficiency in the banking sector. Effective communication with banks will help regulators understand more about the functions and objectives of financial institutions as well as ensure the commitment of banks to prudential measures. Finally, in order to ensure financial stability, in-depth research on financial networks should be strongly supported by central bankers and financial regulators in the region. In today's globally integrated world, it is essential to facilitate multilateral surveillance on economic and financial development.

We have demonstrated that interconnectivity and solvency contagion risk in the banking systems in response to external shocks have declined significantly since 2013, despite the rapid growth in cross-border exposures in value terms. Nonetheless, due to their large size and interconnectedness (i.e., their importance as a financial intermediator), SIBs are found to be more susceptible to induce contagion within the network. In assessing potential losses arising from contagion induced by external shocks, we incorporated two other channels of contagion that are often disregarded in similar counterfactual simulation studies: (i) valuation losses due to common asset exposures and (ii) mark-to-market losses resulting from credit quality deterioration or a loss of confidence (also known as 'credit quality channel':, Fink et al. (2016)).

Results show differences in funding, asset and liability structures between foreign and domestic banks that could affect the relevance and efficacy of policy measures. Policymakers and concerned multilateral agencies may need to revisit capital flow policies and the regulatory mix between domestic and foreign banks to effectively address the challenges of a globally integrated financial market.

The economies within the region surpassed the importance of many of the G7 countries (the UK and Japan, in particular). Since 2016, we observe the dominance of Hong Kong and China in the system. This type of structural change will necessarily have implications for system stability, not only in terms of regional stability but also on a global scale. The dominance of Hong Kong and its extensive links with China are remarkable but not surprising. Nevertheless, this extremely close link could have serious contagion effects if the Chinese economy faces turbulence. Our network analysis shows that the flows of money terminate in China and are not diversified further. This is very different from the 2000s, when Japan played the key role in the network. At that time, the flows of money from Japan were directed mainly at Singapore, but Singapore widely diversified the received financial resources further. Based on our results, there is a need to further explore economies' (banks') portfolio diversification in the region.

We also conclude that a more comprehensive analysis of contagion risk with the help of more complex methodological frameworks can be conducted only if the reported statistics are improved, as studies capable of detecting possible triggers of systemic risk require much more disaggregated statistical information.

# Appendix

**Table A1** List of Economies

| Economy | Abbreviation | Type (Core/ periphery) | Sample period (Core economy) |
|---|---|---|---|
| Australia | AU | C | 1998 Q1–2018 Q1 |
| Bangladesh | BD | P | - |
| Canada | CA | C | 2007 Q3–2018 Q1 |
| China | CN | P | - |
| Hong Kong, SAR | HK | C | 2014 Q4–2018 Q1 |
| India | IN | P | - |
| Indonesia | ID | P | - |
| Japan | JP | C | 1998 Q1–2018 Q1 |
| Macau, SAR | MO | C | 2004 Q1–2018q1 |
| Malaysia | MY | P | - |
| Myanmar | MM | P | - |
| Nepal | NP | P | - |
| New Zealand | NZ | P | - |
| Pakistan | PK | P | - |
| Philippines | PH | C | 2016 Q4–2018 Q1 |
| Singapore | SG | P | - |
| South Korea | KR | C | 2005 Q1–2018 Q1 |
| Sri Lanka | LK | P | - |
| Chinese Taipei | TW | C | 2000 Q4–2018 Q1 |
| Thailand | TH | P | - |
| UK | GB | C | 1998 Q1–2018 Q1 |
| US | US | C | 1998 Q1–2018 Q1 |
| Vietnam | VN | P | - |
| Germany | DE | C | 1998 Q1–2018 Q1 |
| France | FR | C | 1998 Q1–2018 Q1 |
| Italy | IT | C | 2014 Q4–2018 Q1 |
| Switzerland | CH | C | 1998 Q1–2018 Q1 |
| Luxembourg | LU | C | 1998 Q1–2018 Q1 |

**Notes:** C denotes core (reporting) economies of which the data for individual counterparty economies are available, P denotes periphery (non-reporting) economies.

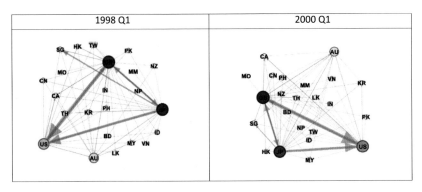

**Figure A1a**

**Notes:** 1998 Q1: Core countries with an individual counterparty include AU, CA, HK, JP, GB, US (Total number of countries: 6)

**Notes:** 2000 Q1: Core countries with an individual counterparty include AU, CA, HK, JP, GB, US (Total number of countries: 6)

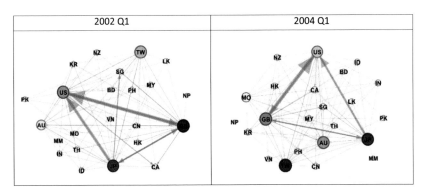

**Figure A1b**

**Notes:** 2002 Q1: Core countries with an individual counterparty include AU, CA, HK, JP, TW, GB, US (Total number of countries: 7)

**Notes:** 2004 Q1: Core countries with an individual counterparty include AU, CA, HK, JP, MO, TW, GB, US (Total number of countries: 8)

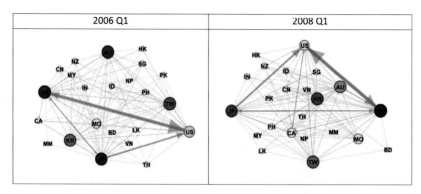

**Figure A1c**

**Notes:** 2006 Q1: Core countries with an individual counterparty include AU, CA, HK, JP, MO, KR, TW, GB, US (Total number of countries: 9)

**Notes:** 2008 Q1: Core countries with an individual counterparty include AU, CA, HK, JP, MO, KR, TW, GB, US (Total number of countries: 9)

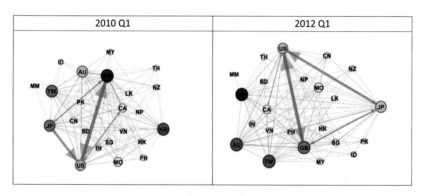

**Figure A1d**

**Notes:** 2010 Q1: Core countries with an individual counterparty include AU, CA, HK, JP, MO, KR, TW, GB, US (Total number of countries: 9)

**Notes:** 2012 Q1: Core countries with an individual counterparty include AU, CA, HK, JP, MO, KR, TW, GB, US (Total number of countries: 9)

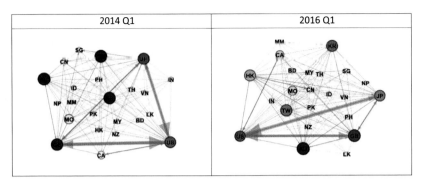

**Figure A1e**

**Notes:** 2014 Q1: Core countries with an individual counterparty include AU, CA, HK, JP, MO, KR, TW, GB, US (Total number of countries: 9)

**Notes:** 2016 Q1: Core countries with an individual counterparty include AU, CA, HK, JP, MO, KR, TW, GB, US (Total number of countries: 9)

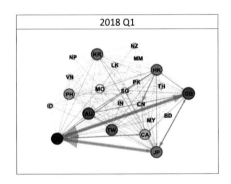

**Figure A1f**

**Notes:** 2018 Q1: Core countries with an individual counterparty include AU, CA, HK, JP, MO, PH, KR, TW, GB, US (Total number of countries: 10)

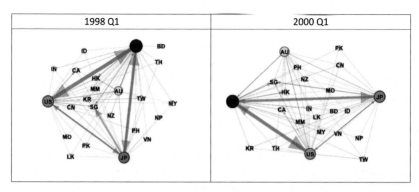

**Figure A2a**

**Notes:** 1998 Q1: Core countries with an individual counterparty include AU, CA, HK, JP, UK, US (Total number of countries: 6)

**Notes:** 2000 Q1: Core countries with an individual counterparty include AU, CA, HK, JP, UK, US (Total number of countries: 6)

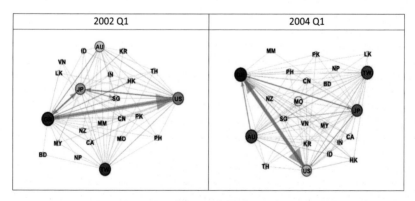

**Figure A2b**

**Notes:** 2002 Q1: Core countries with an individual counterparty include AU, CA, HK, JP, TW, UK, US (Total number of countries: 7)

**Notes:** 2004 Q1: Core countries with an individual counterparty include AU, CA, HK, JP, MO, TW, UK, US (Total number of countries: 8)

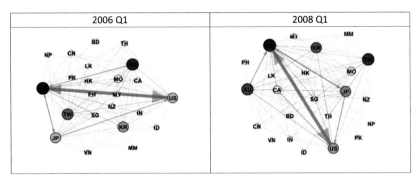

**Figure A2c**

**Notes:** 2006 Q1: Core countries with an individual counterparty include AU, CA, HK, JP, MO, KR, TW, UK, US (Total number of countries: 9)

**Notes:** 2008 Q1: Core countries with an individual counterparty include AU, CA, HK, JP, MO, KR, TW, UK, US (Total number of countries: 9)

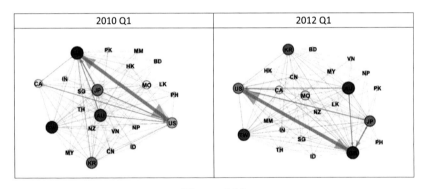

**Figure A2d**

**Notes:** 2010 Q1: Core countries with an individual counterparty include AU, CA, HK, JP, MO, KR, TW, UK, US (Total number of countries: 9)

**Notes:** 2012 Q1: Core countries with an individual counterparty include AU, CA, HK, JP, MO, KR, TW, UK, US (Total number of countries: 9)

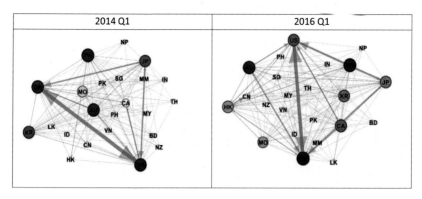

**Figure A2e**

**Notes:** 2014 Q1: Core countries with an individual counterparty include AU, CA, HK, JP, MO, KR, TW, UK, US (Total number of countries: 9)

**Notes:** 2016 Q1: Core countries with an individual counterparty include AU, CA, HK, JP, MO, KR, TW, UK, US (Total number of countries: 9)

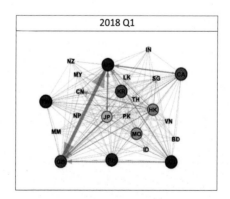

**Figure A2f**

**Notes:** 2018 Q1: Core countries with an individual counterparty include AU, CA, HK, JP, MO, PH, KR, TW, UK, US (Total number of countries: 10)

# References

Aba, L. A. (2019), 'Cross-Border Interbank Contagion Risk Analysis for Papua New Guinea'. In R. Matousek (ed.), Cross-Border Interbank Contagion Risk Analysis. Kuala Lumpur: The SEACEN Centre, pp. 109–42.

Adekola, A., and B. S. Sergi (2016), Global Business Management: A Cross-Cultural Perspective. New York: Routledge.

Agenor, P.-R. (2003), 'Benefits and Costs of International Financial Integration: Theory and Facts', *The World Economy*, Vol. 26, no. 8, pp.1089–118.

Ahrend, R., J. Arnold and F. Murtin (2011), 'Have More Strictly Regulated Banking Systems Fared Better during the Recent Financial Crisis?' *Applied Economics Letters*, Vol. 18, no. 5, pp. 399–403.

Ahrend, R., and A. Goujard (2011), 'Drivers of Systemic Banking Crises: The Role of Bank-Balance-Sheet Contagion and Financial Account Structure', *OECD Economics Department Working Papers*, no. 902, OECD Publishing.

Ahrend, R., and A. Goujard (2012), 'International Capital Mobility and Financial Fragility – Part 3. How Do Structural Policies Affect Financial Crisis Risk?: Evidence from Past Crises across OECD and Emerging Economies', *OECD Economics Department Working Papers*, no. 966, OECD Publishing, available at http://dx.doi.org/10.1787/5k97fmtj5vtk-en.

Ahrend, R., and C. Schwellnus (2012), 'Which Structural Policies Stabilise Capital Flows When Investors Suddenly Change Their Mind? Evidence from Bilateral Bank Data', *OECD Economics Department Working Papers*, no. 967, OECD Publishing.

Allen, F., and D. Gale (2000), 'Financial Contagion', Journal of Political Economy, Vol. 108, no. 1, pp.1–33.

Aoyama, H., S. Battiston and Y. Fujiwara (2013), 'DebtRank Analysis of the Japanese Credit Network', *RIETI Discussion Paper Series*, 13-E-087, available at www.rieti.go.jp/jp/publications/dp/13e087.pdf

Bank Negara Malaysia (2013), 'Financial Stability and Payment Systems Report', Bank Negara Malaysia, pp. 46–51, available at www.bnm.gov.my /index.php?ch=en_publication&pg=en_fspr&ac=8&lang=en.

Bardoscia, M., P. Barucca, C. A. Brinley and J. Hill (2017), 'The Decline of Solvency Contagion Risk', *Bank of England Staff Working Paper*, 662.

Bardoscia, M., S. Battiston, F. Caccioli and G. Caldarelli (2015), 'DebtRank: A Microscopic Foundation for Shock Propagation', *PLOS One*, Vol. 10, no. 6, p.e0130406.

Bardoscia, M., F. Caccioli, J. Perotti, G. Vivaldo and G. Caldarelli (2016), 'Distress Propagation in Complex Networks: The Case of Non-Linear DebtRank', *PLOS One*, Vol. 11, no. 10, p. e0163825.

Battiston, S., G. Caldarelli, M. D'Errico and S. Gurciullo (2016), 'Leveraging the network: A stress-test framework based on DebtRank', Statistics & Risk Modeling, Volume 33: Issue 3–4, pp.117–138.

Battiston, S., D. Delli Gatti, M. Gallegati, B. Greenwald and J. Stiglitz (2012), 'Liaisons Dangereuses: Increasing Connectivity, Risk Sharing, and Systemic Risk', *Journal of Economic Dynamics and Control*, Vol. 36, no. 8, pp. 1121–41.

Battiston, S., M. Puliga, R. Kaushik, P. Tasca and G. Caldarelliet (2012), 'DebtRank: Too Central to Fail? Financial Networks, the FED and Systemic Risk', *Scientific Report* 2, no 1, 541.

BIS (2011), "Global systemically important banks: assessment methodology and the additional loss absorbency requirement - Rule Text," BIS Basel Committee on Banking Supervision, November.

Borio, C. (2014), 'The International Monetary and Financial System: Its Achilles Heel and What to Do about It', *BIS Working Papers*, no. 456, September.

Borio, C., and P. Disyatat (2011), 'Global Imbalances and the Financial Crisis: Link or No Link?' *BIS Working Papers*, no. 346, May; revised and extended version of 'Global Imbalances and the Financial Crisis: Reassessing the Role of International Finance', *Asian Economic Policy Review*, Vol. 5, 2010, pp.198–216.

Borio, C., H. James and H. S. Shin (2014), 'The International Monetary and Financial System: A Capital Account Historical Perspective', *BIS Working Papers*, 457, Bank for International Settlements, available at www.bis.org /publ/work457.pdf.

Boss, M., H. Elsinger, M. Summer and S. Thurner (2004), 'Network Topology of the Interbank Market', *Quantitative Finance*, Vol. 4, no. 6, pp. 677–84.

Burrows, O., D. Learmonth, J. McKeown and R. Williams (2012), 'RAMSI: A Top-Down Stress-Testing Model Developed at the Bank of England', *Quarterly Bulletin*, 2012 Q3, Bank of England, pp. 204–10, available at www .bankofengland.co.uk/-/media/boe/files/quarterly-bulletin/2012/ramsi-a-top-down-stress-testing-model-developed-at-the-boe.pdf.

Cerutti, E. (2015), 'Drivers of Cross-Border Banking Exposures during the Crisis', *Journal of Banking and Finance*, Vol. 55, pp. 340–75.

Cerutti, E., S. Claessens and P. McGuire (2012), 'Systemic Risks in Global Banking: What Available Data Can Tell Us and What More Data Are Needed?' *NBER Working Paper*, no. 18531.

Changmo, A., G. Lee and D. Chang (2014), 'The Global Financial Crisis and Transmission Channels: An International Network Analysis', *Working Paper*

*7/2014*, The South East Asian Central Banks (SEACEN) Research and Training Centre, Kuala Lumpur, Malaysia.

Chan-Lau, J., M. Espinosa, K. Giesecke and J. Solé (2009), 'Assessing the Systemic Implications of Financial Linkages', IMF Global Financial Stability Report, 2, April.

Cho, D., and Changyong R. (2013), 'Effects of Quantitative Easing on Asia: Capital Flows and Financial Markets', *ADB Economics Working Paper Series*, no. 350.

Cihák, M., and L. L. Ong (2007), 'Estimating Spillover Risk among Large EU Banks', *IMF Working Paper*, European Department and Monetary and Capital Markets Department.

Degryse, H., and G. Nguyễn (2004), 'Interbank Exposures: An Empirical Examination of Systemic Risk in the Belgian Interbank Market', *NBB Working Paper*, no. 43.

Dizon, J. T., J. P. Hutalla and J. M. Rariza, Jr. (2019), 'Philippines: Contagion Risk Analysis of Cross-Border Exposures of Banks'. In R. Matousek (ed.), *Cross-Border Interbank Contagion Risk Analysis*. Kuala Lumpur: The SEACEN Centre, pp. 143–174.

Dungey, M., and D. Gajurel (2015), 'Contagion and Banking Crisis – International Evidence for 2007–2009', *Journal of Banking & Finance, Vol.* 60, pp. 271–83.

Elsinger, H., A. Lehar and M. Summer (2012), 'Network Models and Systemic Risk Assessment', available at www.researchgate.net/publication/309187281_N etwork_models_and_systemic_risk_assessment (accessed 7 January 2019).

Espinosa-Vega, M., and J. Solé (2010), 'Cross-Border Financial Surveillance: A Network Perspective', *IMF Working Paper*, 10/105.

Fagiolo, G. (2007), 'Clustering in Complex Directed Networks', *Physical Review E*, Vol. 76, 026107.

Fender, I., and P. McGuire (2010), 'European Banks' US Dollar Funding Pressures', *BIS Quarterly Review*, June, pp. 57–64.

Fink, K., U. Krüger, B. Meller and L. Wong (2016), 'The Credit Quality Channel: Modeling Contagion in the Interbank Market', *Journal of Financial Stability*, Vol. 25, pp. 83–97.

Forbes, K. (2012), 'The "Big C": Identifying and Mitigating Contagion', 36th Jackson Hole Symposium.

Freixas, X., B. Parigi and J.-C. Rochet (2000), 'Systemic Risk, Interbank Relations and Liquidity Provision by the Central Bank', *Journal of Money Credit and Banking*. Vol. 32, pp. 611–38.

Furfine, C. H. (2003), 'Interbank Exposures: Quantifying the Risk of Contagion', *Journal of Money, Credit and Banking*, Vol. 35, no. 1, pp. 111–28.

Gai, P., and S. Kapadia (2010), 'Contagion in Financial Networks', Proceedings of the Royal Statistical Society – Series A: Mathematical, Physical and Engineering Sciences, Vol. 466, no. 2120, pp. 2401–23.

Genberg, H. (2017), 'Global Shocks and Risk to Financial Stability in Asia', *Working Paper 25/2017*, The South East Asian Central Banks (SEACEN) Research and Training Centre, Kuala Lumpur, Malaysia.

Glasserman, P., and H. Young (2015), 'How Likely Is Contagion in Financial Networks?' *Journal of Banking & Finance, Vol.* 50, pp. 383–99.

Goyal, S., and B. S. Sergi (2015). 'Social Entrepreneurship and Sustainability – Understanding the Context and Key Characteristics', *Journal of Security and Sustainability Issues*, Vol. 4, no. 3, pp. 269–78.

Goyal, S., B. S. Sergi and A. Kapoor (2017), 'Emerging Role of For-Profit Social Enterprises at the Base of the Pyramid: The Case of Selco', Journal of Management Development, Vol. 36, no. 1, pp. 97–108.

Group of Ten, Task Force on the Impact of Financial Consolidation on Monetary Policy (2001), Report on Consolidation in the Financial Sector. Basel: Bank for International Settlements.

Haldane, A. G., and R. M. May (2011), 'Systemic Risk in Banking Ecosystems', *Nature*, Vol. 469, pp. 351–55.

Hattori, M., and Y. Suda (2007), 'Developments in a Cross-Border Bank Exposure Network', *Bank of Japan Working Paper*, no. 07-E-21.

Herd, R., V. Koen, I. Patnaik and A.Shah (2011), 'Financial Sector Reform in India: Time for a Second Wave?', *Economics Department Working Papers*, no. 879. OECD, Paris, France.

Hoggarth, G., L. Mahadeva and J. Martin (2010), 'Understanding International Bank Capital Flows during the Recent Financial Crisis', *Financial Stability Paper*, no. 8, Bank of England.

Hoggarth, G., R. Reis and V. Saporta (2001), 'Costs of Banking System Instability: Some Empirical Evidence', *Journal of Banking and Finance*, Vol. 26, pp.825–55.

Kolaczyk, E. D. (2009), Statistical Analysis of Network Data: Methods and Models. New York: Springer-Verlag.

Korniyenko, Y., M. Patnam, R. M. del Rio-Chanon and M. A. Porter (2018), 'Evolution of the Global Financial Network and Contagion: A New Approach', *IMF Working Papers*, 18/113, International Monetary Fund.

Kubelec, C. and F. Sa, 2010, "The geographical composition of national external balance sheets: 1980–2005," Bank of England Working Paper No. 384.

Lee, S. (2019), 'Global Network in Cross-Border Interbank Flows: The Case of South Korea'. In R. Matousek (ed.), Cross-Border Interbank Contagion Risk Analysis. Kuala Lumpur: The SEACEN Centre, pp. 63–82.

Leitner, Y. (2005), 'Financial Networks: Contagion, Commitment, and Private Sector Bailouts', *Journal of Finance*, Vol. 60, pp. 2925–53.

Matousek, R. (2019), *Cross-Border Interbank Contagion Risk Analysis*. Kuala Lumpur: The SEACEN Centre.

Matousek, R., H. Lee and O. Rummel (2019), 'Contagion Risk Analysis through Visual Network: An Overview of the Asia-Pacific Region'. In R. Matousek (ed.), *Cross-Border Interbank Contagion Risk Analysis*. Kuala Lumpur: The SEACEN Centre, pp. 9–38.

McGuire, P., and P. Wooldridge (2005), 'The BIS Consolidated Banking Statistics: Structure, Uses and Recent Enhancements', *BIS Quarterly Review*, September.

Minoiu, C., and J. A. Reyes (2013), 'A Network Analysis of Global Banking: 19782010', *Journal of Financial Stability*, Vol. 9, no. 2, pp. 168–84.

Muhajir, M. H., A. H. F. Wibowo and I. Ramdhani (2019), 'Understanding Cross-Border Contagion Risk in Indonesia'. In R. Matousek (ed.), *Cross-Border Interbank Contagion Risk Analysis*. Kuala Lumpur: The SEACEN Centre, pp. 39–62.

Narasimham, M. (1991), Report of the Committee on *the F*inancial *S*ystem. Mumbai: Reserve Bank of India.

Narasimham, M. (1998), *Report of the Committee on Banking Sector Reforms*. New Delhi: Ministry of Finance.

Newman, M. (2010), Networks: An Introduction. Oxford: Oxford University Press.

Nguyễn, H. P., H. Phuong, P. M. Cuong and Ngo, HL. (2019), 'Cross Border Interbank Contagion Risk from Vietnam's Banking System'. In R. Matousek (ed.), *Cross-Border Interbank Contagion Risk Analysis*. Kuala Lumpur: The SEACEN Centre, pp. 195–212.

Nier, E., J. Yang, T. Yorulmazer and A. Alentorn (2008), 'Network Models and Financial Stability', *Bank of England Working Paper*, no. 346.

OECD (2012), 'Financial Contagion in the Era of Globalised Banking?' *OECD Economics Department Policy Notes*, June, no. 14.

Onour, I. A., and B. S. Sergi (2010) 'GCC Stock Markets: How Risky Are They?', *International Journal of Monetary Economics and Finance*, Vol. 3, no. 4, pp. 330–37.

Opsahl, T., F. Agneessens and J. Skvoretz (2010), 'Node Centrality in Weighted Networks: Generalizing Degree and Shortest Paths', *Social Networks*, Vol. 32, no. 3, pp. 245–51.

Park, C.-Y., and K. Shin (2017), 'A Contagion through Exposure to Foreign Banks during the Global Financial Crisis', *Asian Development Bank Economics Working Paper Series*, July, no. 516.

Peltonen, T., A. Piloiu and P. Sarlin (2015), 'Network Linkages to Predict Bank Distress', European Central Bank Working Paper Series Number 1828, pp. 1–35.

Qerimi, Q., and B. S. Sergi (2015) 'Development and Social Development in the Global Context', *International Journal of Business and Globalisation*, Vol. 14, no. 4, pp. 383–407.

Remolona, E., and I. Shim (2015), 'The Rise of Regional Banking in Asia and the Pacific', *BIS Quarterly Review*, September, pp. 119–34, available at www .bis.org/publ/qtrpdf/r_qt1509j.pdf (accessed 28 December 2018).

Reyes, J., and C. Minoiu (2011), 'A Network Analysis of Global Banking:1978–2009', *IMF Working Papers*, Vol. 11, no. 74, p. 1.

Sababathy, H., and L S. Ling (2019), 'Cross-Border Interbank Contagion Risk to Malaysian Banking System'. In R. Matousek (ed.), *Cross-Border Interbank Contagion Risk Analysis*. Kuala Lumpur: The SEACEN Centre, pp. 83–108.

Sengupta R., and H. Vardhan (2017), 'This Time It Is Different: Non-performing Assets in Indian Banks', *Economic and Political Weekly*, Vol. 52, no. 12, pp. 85–95.

Sergi, B. S. (2000), 'A New Index of Independence of 12 European National Central Banks: The 1980s and Early 1990s', *Journal of Transnational Management Development*, Vol. 5, no. 2, pp. 41–57.

Sergi, B. S. (2019), Modeling Economic Growth in Contemporary Russia. Bingley, UK: Emerald Publishing.

Sergi, B. S., E. Popkova, A. Bogoviz and J. Ragulina (2019), 'Entrepreneurship and Economic Growth: The Experience of Developed and Developing Countries'. In B. S. Sergi and C. Scanlon (ed.), *Entrepreneurship and Development in the 21st Century* (*Lab for Entrepreneurship and Development*). Bingley, UK: Emerald Publishing, pp. 3–32.

Sharma, U. (2019), 'Cross-Border Banking in Indian Context'. In R. Matousek (ed.), *Cross-Border Interbank Contagion Risk Analysis*. Kuala Lumpur: The SEACEN Centre, pp. 39–62.

Sheldon, G., and M. Maurer (1998), 'Interbank Lending and Systemic Risk: An Empirical Analysis for Switzerland', *Swiss Journal of Economics and Statistics*, Vol. 134, pp. 685–704.

Smaga, P. (2014), 'The Concept of Systemic Risk', SRC Special Paper, no. 5.

Summer, M. (2013), 'Financial Contagion and Network Analysis', *Annual Review of Financial Economics*, Vol. 5, no. 1, pp. 277–97.

Tabak, B. M., S. Souza and S. Guerra (2013), 'Assessing Systemic Risk in the Brazilian Interbank Market', *Banco Central do Brasil Working Papers*, no. 318.

Tabak, B. M., M. Takami, J. M. C. Rocha and D. O. Cajueiro (2011), 'Directed Clustering Coefficient as a Measure of Systemic Risk in Complex Banking Networks', *Banco Central do Brasil Working Papers*, no. 249.

Tonzer, L. (2015), 'Cross-Border Interbank Networks, Banking Risk and Contagion', *Journal of Financial Stability*, Vol. 18, Issue C, pp. 5.

Upper, C. (2007), 'Using Counterfactual Simulations to Assess the Danger of Contagion in Interbank Markets', *BIS Working Paper*, no. 234.

Upper, C. (2011), 'Simulation Methods to Assess the Danger of Contagion in Interbank Markets', *Journal of Financial Stability*, Vol. 7, No. 3, pp. 111–25.

Upper, C., and A. Worms (2004), 'Estimating Bilateral Exposures in the German Interbank Market: Is There a Danger of Contagion?' *European Economic Review*, Vol. 48, no. 4, pp. 827–49.

Von Peter, G. (2007), 'International Banking Centres: A Network Perspective', *BIS Quarterly Review Working Paper*, Basel, Switzerland.

Watts, D. J., and S. H. Strogatz (1998), 'Collective Dynamics of 'Small-World' Networks', *Nature*, Vol. 393, pp. 440–42.

Wells, S. (2004), 'Financial Interlinkages in the United Kingdom's Interbank Market and the Risk of Contagion', Bank of England Working Paper, no. 230.

Yellen, J. (2013), 'Interconnectedness and Systemic Risk: Lessons from the Financial Crisis and Policy Implications',*Board of Governors of the Federal Reserve System*, Washington, D.C.

Yilmaz, K. (2017), *Bank Volatility Connectedness in the SEACEN Region*. Kuala Lumpur: SEACEN.

# Acknowledgements

The authors would like to acknowledge the contributions of the research teams from seven central banks located in the Asia-Pacific region – namely, the Reserve Bank of India, Bank Indonesia, Bank of Korea, Bank Negara Malaysia, Bank of Papua New Guinea, Bangko Sentral ng Pilipinas and State Bank of Vietnam – who participated in the research project on 'Cross-Border Interbank Contagion Risk Analysis' at the SEACEN Centre, Kuala Lumpur, Malaysia. The authors thank Upasana Sharma (Reserve Bank of India), Maulana Harris Muhajir, Arnanda H. F. Wibowo and Irman Ramdhani (Bank Indonesia), Harikumara Sababathy and Lim Sheng Ling (Bank Negara Malays), Ludwig Aur Aba (Bank of Papua New Guinea), Jenny Dizon, Jessica Hutalla and Jamie Rariza Jr. (Bangko Sentral ng Pilipinas), and Nguyen Ha Phuong, Phan Manh Cuong and Ngo Ti Huyen Linh (State Bank of Vietnam) for their contributions to the research output. The authors are further particularly grateful to Seohyun Lee (International Monetary Fund) for her excellent research support and visual network analyses.

## Cambridge Elements ☰

# Economics of Emerging Markets

## Bruno S. Sergi
*Harvard University*

Editor Bruno S. Sergi is an Instructor at Harvard University, an Associate of the Harvard University Davis Center for Russian and Eurasian Studies and Harvard Ukrainian Research Institute. He is the Academic Series Editor of the Cambridge *Elements in the Economics of Emerging Markets* (Cambridge University Press), a co-editor of the *Lab for Entrepreneurship and Development* book series, and associate editor of *The American Economist*. Concurrently, he teaches International Economics at the University of Messina, Scientific Director of the Lab for Entrepreneurship and Development (LEAD), and a co-founder and Scientific Director of the International Center for Emerging Markets Research at RUDN University in Moscow. He has published over 150 articles in professional journals and twenty-one books as author, co-author, editor, and co-editor.

## About the Series
The aim of this Elements series is to deliver state-of-the-art, comprehensive coverage of the knowledge developed to date, including the dynamics and prospects of these economies, focusing on emerging markets' economics, finance, banking, technology advances, trade, demographic challenges, and their economic relations with the rest of the world, as well as the causal factors and limits of economic policy in these markets.

**Cambridge Elements** ⹀

# Economics of Emerging Markets

Printed in the United States
By Bookmasters